Loan Risk Management of Commercial Real Estate Debt Funds

Wilhelm Hammel

Loan Risk Management of Commercial Real Estate Debt Funds

Springer Gabler

Wilhelm Hammel
Department of Real Estate Economics
and Management
HAWK University of Applied Science
and Arts
Holzminden, Germany

ISBN 978-3-658-48911-3 ISBN 978-3-658-48912-0 (eBook)
https://doi.org/10.1007/978-3-658-48912-0

This Springer Gabler imprint is published by the registered company Springer Fachmedien Wiesbaden GmbH, part of Springer Nature.
The registered company address is: Abraham-Lincoln-Str. 46, 65189 Wiesbaden, Germany

Indeed, better risk management may be the only truly necessary element of success in banking.

(Alan Greenspan, Chairperson: US Federal Reserve System, 1987–2006 (b. 1926))

Disclaimer

This academic research study was submitted by the author in November 2024 to SDA Bocconi (Milan, Italy) in fulfilment of the requirements for the degree of Doctor of Business Administration (DBA).

To enhance readability, minor revisions have been made for this print edition, primarily involving the removal of encoded references to interviewees within the text. Instead, anonymised direct quotes are used to indicate interviewee group categories.

As the interviews are integral to the DBA thesis, the identities of interview participants were encrypted in a separate document, exclusively accessible to SDA Bocconi's review commission, in compliance with academic research standards and data protection regulations.

Contents

Acronyms and Initialisms

AIF	alternative investment fund
AIFM	alternative investment fund manager
AIFMD	Alternative Investment Fund Managers Directive
AUM	assets under management
BaFin	Bundesanstalt für Finanzdienstleistungsaufsicht
BCBS	Basel Committee on Banking Supervision
BIS	Bank for International Settlements
CapEx	capital expenditure
CRD	Capital Requirements Directive
CRE	commercial real estate
CRR	capital requirements regulation
DBA	Doctor of Business Administration
DSCR	debt service cover ratio
EBA	European Banking Authority
ECB	European Central Bank
ECL	expected credit loss
EIOPA	European Insurance and Occupational Pensions Authority
EPRA	European Real Estate Association
ESG	environmental, social and governance
ESMA	European Securities and Markets Authority
ESRB	European Systemic Risk Board
EU	European Union
EUR	Euros
Eurostat	Statistical Office of the European Union

FDIC	Federal Deposit Insurance Corporation
GDP	gross domestic product
GFC	global financial crisis
ICR	interest cover ratio
IMF	International Monetary Fund
INREV	European Association for Investors in Non-Listed Real Estate Vehicles
KPI	key performance indicator
LTV	loan-to-value
NPL	non-performing loan
o. i.	own illustration
OCC	Office of the Comptroller of the Currency
PGIM	Prudential Global Investment Management
PL	performing loan
RRE	residential real estate
SPL	sub-performing loan
SPV	special purpose vehicle
UCTIS	Undertakings for Collective Investment in Transferable Securities Directive
UK	United Kingdom
US	United States of America
VDP	Verband Deutscher Pfandbriefbanken
WoS	Web of Science

List of Figures

List of Tables

1 Introduction

In recent years, a largely unexpected series of global crises has had a significant impact on the global property market. Commercial real estate (CRE) was hit particularly hard by the Covid-19 pandemic. The value of office space began to erode, as working remotely became commonplace and office vacancy rates increased. Equally, the demand for retail space decreased, as many employees moved out of the city in search of larger homes in greener areas, and consequently more frequently opted for online shopping. The rapid and persistent increase in e-commerce, which was already evident before the widespread imposition of lockdowns as public health responses during the pandemic, left shopping malls and city centres empty. While business travel retained its importance in the corporate world, accelerated digital transformation and the green agenda both appeared to restrict it to so-called business-critical trips, and it was widely expected that occupancy rates of business and conference hotels would not recover to pre-pandemic levels. Moreover, the Russian war of aggression against Ukraine sent geopolitical shockwaves throughout the global economy, leading to significant volatility in financial and energy markets. These wider macroeconomic developments had consequences for the CRE market, as the sharp increase in interest rates made refinancing costly, rendering CRE lenders more cautious. Consequently, the volume of available loans and transactions, and hence values, was reduced.

The German expression *Betongold* ("concrete gold") suggests that real estate is as valuable as gold and as durable as concrete. This assumption has frequently prompted investors to undertake risky ventures. However, it has proven to be overly optimistic, as in reality there has been a periodic recurrence in economic cycles of so-called black swan events (however technically inaccurate this designation might be). Although a black swan event might be unpredicted and unexpected, it is typically not entirely unprecedented. This observation raises the

W. Hammel, *Loan Risk Management of Commercial Real Estate Debt Funds*,
https://doi.org/10.1007/978-3-658-48912-0_1

question of whether the CRE industry has learnt its lessons and, in anticipation of such events in the future, has expanded its capacity to better withstand or rapidly recover from economic crises—in other words, to enhance its resilience.

In expectation of relatively high accessibility, fairly stable returns, and reasonable safety, investors such as occupational pension funds and insurance companies increasingly invested in CRE debt funds. It seems that debt funds were regarded as less risky than equity funds and more profitable than government bonds or bank deposits. The goal of this study was to explore the extent to which these CRE debt funds were able to weather the storm by wisely adopting effective loan risk management procedures and processes.

Based on these preliminary considerations, the research object of this thesis, the underlying research problem, and the derived purpose statement are introduced. To guide the reader through this document, which is roughly based on the sequential steps of the research process, the structure of the thesis is outlined in this introductory chapter.

1.1 Research Object

Following these preliminary considerations, the research object is presented, followed by the purpose statement, which is derived from the given research problem.

The research object was loan risk management practices of CRE debt funds and their plausible effects on loan performance. In Europe, CRE debt funds rose to prominence in the wake of the 2007–2008 global financial crisis (GFC), which was widely regarded as the most severe worldwide economic crisis since the Great Depression that blighted the 1930s. Following regulatory changes and increased liquidity requirements, banks and other more traditional capital lending sources were forced to either reduce CRE lending or to become cash flow lenders, as opposed to asset-based lenders. The downturn in CRE bank loans opened the door for alternative lenders challenging traditional banking practices.

The geographic focus of the research study was on the United Kingdom (UK) and Germany, which are the two largest real estate markets in Europe. Together, in Europe, they accounted for approximately 36% of the gross domestic product (GDP) and 40% of CRE stock in 2020 as per the report of the European Real Estate Association (EPRA, 2021), and about 50% of CRE transactions in 2022, with the UK totalling about 65 billion Euros (EUR) in CRE transactions and Germany 54 billion EUR, respectively (BNP Paribas Real Estate, 2023). This geographic delimitation avoided the high degree of complexity which would otherwise have resulted from the various legal and tax regimes in place across Europe. It was expected, however, that a broader spectrum of debt funds qualified for geographic categorisation under this research focus. In particular, debt funds were deemed to focus on the UK or Germany if they were based or predominately investing in either of these countries. The latter was the case for many debt funds incorporated in Luxembourg (KPMG, 2022; Loyens & Loeff, 2022), which consequently played a larger role in this research study than the geographic delimitation suggested.

The temporal focus from the end of 2021 to the completion of data collection in mid-2024 was selected for two main reasons. Firstly, institutional memory in companies was frequently limited, usually due to personnel fluctuations, and allowance was made for the tendency of interviewees to focus on more recent events. Secondly, the massive impact on financial and property markets of the global Covid-19 pandemic and the consequences of Russia's war on Ukraine were considered. However, this temporal delimitation should not suggest a particular focus on the chronological sequence of events. Rather, the study was focussed on addressing questions about relevant processes and mechanisms, and their consequences during the period under review.

1.2 Research Problem and Purpose Statement

In this section, the research problem is introduced by a brief discussion of loan risk management of CRE debt funds. While a scientific study should be introduced by a presentation of the research problem, this presentation must be preceded by a brief discussion of CRE debt fund loan risk management. The definition of key concepts and technical terms, and the presentation of the current state of research will both only be given in the following chapters. The same applies to the purpose statement, which was derived from the research problem and summarises the research objectives, thereby providing a basic understanding of the topic the study covers.

As specialised investment companies, CRE debt funds enable professional investors to engage with the CRE market, thereby capitalising from the gradual post-GFC retreat of banks and other more traditional capital sources from the CRE lending space (PGIM, 2021a). In this way, debt funds filled the gap created by stricter banking regulation and supervision, as banks became more risk-averse due to the capital rules and risk weightings that were introduced. By connecting borrowers with capital provided by professional investors such as occupational pension funds and insurance companies, CRE debt funds occupy a particular niche in the sphere of CRE lending. The fact that the alternative CRE lending space is regarded as more manageable in terms of the numbers and typical sizes of participating companies as evidenced in two reports by European Association for Investors in Non-Listed Real Estate Vehicles (INREV) in 2023 (INREV, 2023a) and 2024 (INREV, 2024) makes debt funds a valid field for academic research. At the same time, the company sizes of smaller debt funds, in particular, which have limited human and financial resources, might pose specific challenges for effective operational processes. This applies above all to loan risk management—the focus of this study. CRE debt funds fall outside the scope of the much larger so-called TBTF (too-big-to-fail) financial institutions, whose failure would be considered disastrous for the greater economic system. As argued, unlike banks that manage customer deposits, debt funds are not subject to strict regulatory supervision and publicity requirements. The observed tendency of CRE debt funds to invest in asset classes, geographic regions and capital structures from which traditional financial institutions withdrew might have exposed them to wider risk potential. The study explored to what extent alternative lenders were exposed to increased levels of credit risk due to (i) higher allocation of riskier loans; (ii) limited portfolios with little headroom for loan-by-loan balancing off of losses; and (iii) personnel resource constraints arising from their being relatively smaller than traditional financial institutions. The combination of these variables made loan risk management in the alternative lending space not merely interesting, but also a field urgently requiring academic research.

This study aimed at exploring the extent to which CRE debt funds were able, with foresight, to position themselves ahead of the curve by adopting effective loan risk management procedures and processes. The focus was on the plausible effects of loan risk management practices on loan performance. As the alternative lending space only rose to prominence in the wake of the GFC, CRE debt funds are still regarded as a novel, relatively recent phenomenon in the European CRE loan space. For this reason, as outlined in the literature review synopsis in Chap. 3, this area so far remained virtually untouched by academic research.

Given the huge impact on the CRE market of the recent series of global crises, most notably the Covid-19 pandemic and the macroeconomic consequences of Russia's war on Ukraine, shedding light on the rather opaque alternative lending space appeared to be more urgent than ever. This investigation seemed even more timely in the light of the detailed compromise text for the Alternative Investment Fund Managers Directive (European Parliament, Directive 2024/927—AIFMD II, 2024) enacted into European Law in 2024 after several years of negotiations. Loans are now subject to detailed additional restrictions in relation to leverage limits and risk management. This research was also conducted against the backdrop of the increased significance of risks associated with non-compliance with environmental, social and governance (ESG) regulations. The environmental regulations are often referred to as "green transition". CRE debt funds might increasingly direct their lending efforts towards ESG-accredited projects, which might be easier to finance under better credit terms. They might also in the future be prompted by regulatory authorities to publish loan-by-loan data, which will be required for verifying compliance with ESG regulations. As the focus of the study was on the credit risks to which CRE debt funds are exposed, ESG compliance risks were only examined in cases where they constituted loan-level credit risks. The transformational processes of the lenders themselves to more climate-neutral enterprises against the backdrop of the green transition were beyond the scope of this research.

The findings of this research study are deemed to be of potential interest to academic researchers, practitioners, lawmakers, and financial regulators alike. The novelty argument was largely based on the evident gap in academic research on this rather opaque sector, characterised by the limited publicly available quantitative data. By examining causal links between loan risk management practices and loan performance, this research aimed at bridging this gap through a mechanism-oriented qualitative research approach.

1.3 Structure of the Thesis

The structure of this thesis follows the logical sequence of the research process, as it was implemented in iterative steps between mid-2022 and the latter part of 2024.

The theoretical framework and the conceptual model used for this research study are presented in Chap. 2. To provide the reader with theoretical classifications that apply to the following chapters of this thesis, key concepts and technical terms are defined.

Following this basic exposition of concepts and terms, Chap. 3 provides a summarised discussion of the current state of research, primarily peer-reviewed academic writings as discussed in the author's earlier literature review synopsis (Hammel, 2022). As relevant sources besides peer-reviewed academic literature proved to be of particular interest for the desk study, these are also discussed.

Chapter 4 presents the central research question and sub-questions as they emerged from the research gaps that were identified as key findings of the academic literature review. Having been further developed from the initial research proposal (Hammel, 2023), verifiable ex-ante propositions providing predictions of the research outcomes are also presented. Interrelations between these concepts, that form the building blocks of the suggested theory, are outlined.

Chapter 5 presents the research design and methodologies which were considered appropriate to respond to the research questions and to test and verify or reject the ex-ante propositions. This chapter presents a concise and updated version of the author's initial research proposal; the qualitative research approach is outlined, and arguments for choosing grounded theory for the research design are presented. The method of non-random, purposeful sample selection for semi-structured interviews is introduced, and target group-specific interview guidelines are discussed. Thereafter, data management and data analysis processes are outlined.

The research findings are presented in Chap. 6. The first two subchapters focus on the core dimensions of the two-staged central research question. As the mechanism-oriented investigation should do justice to the complexity of the processes involved, these subchapters are further structured into sections that are oriented towards key criteria and underlying assessment dimensions. Keeping the possibility of multicausality in mind, causal mechanisms were tested, ex-ante propositions verified, and a comparative analysis presented. The third subchapter includes the findings of a small-scale survey which aimed at complementing the open-ended qualitative research with a graphical illustration of respondents' opinions and perceptions. The fourth subchapter presents a brief reflective excursus, focusing on wider economic impacts.

Finally, Chap. 7 summarises the novel contribution of this research study to academic debate, and by way of conclusion, responds to the empirical research questions. Complexity is thereby reduced, and key findings are consolidated to allow for a plausible verification of the assumed causal mechanisms. Derived implications for management practice, for regulatory supervision, and for academic debate in the researched field are presented.

1.3 Structure of the Thesis

Key Concepts and Technical Terms 2

In this section, the theoretical framework and the conceptual model used for this research study are presented. While CRE and related terms are widely used in academic debate and economic practice, the understanding of the underlying concepts and related terminology seems to lack uniformity. To address such imprecision and to provide the reader with consistent theoretical classifications that apply to the following chapters, key concepts and technical terms must be defined. Apart from the basic understanding of CRE and its demarcation from residential real estate (RRE), these concepts and terms include CRE lending and the CRE debt fund universe; loan performance and loss minimisation; and lender-level and loan-level risk management.

2.1 Commercial Real Estate vs Residential Real Estate

Real estate is the largest non-financial asset class in the world. According to the current affairs weekly *The Economist* (The Economist, 2022), in 2022 it made up approximately 68% of the world's nonfinancial assets including plants and machinery, as well as intangibles such as intellectual property. Land alone, excluding the structures built on it, accounted for slightly over half of that share. In recent years, as the value of land has surged, the share of land as a proportion of nonfinancial assets has increased sharply in some countries. In Britain, for instance, it rose from 39% in 1995 to 56% in 2020.

Real estate can be divided into two broad categories: RRE and CRE. According to the classification of the capital requirements regulation (CRR) of the European Regulation in article 4 (75), residential property is defined as a residence, occupied by the owner or the lessee, including apartments in housing cooperatives. The European Systemic Risk Board (ESRB) further specified that

W. Hammel, *Loan Risk Management of Commercial Real Estate Debt Funds*,
https://doi.org/10.1007/978-3-658-48912-0_2

RRE includes buy-to-let housing, which is typically undertaken by private landlords (ESRB, 2019b). In contrast, rental housing leased to a tenant by professional landlords, such as housing companies, is defined as CRE.

The term CRE is not as clearly defined as RRE, as the conceptual understanding seems to vary from country to country and from agency to agency (ESRB, 2019b). Notwithstanding the differing interpretations of the terminology, the ESRB stated that although CRE was a crucial sector from a risk perspective, it remained underrepresented in statistical systems. To establish conceptual consistency, the ESRB provided the following definition:

> *CRE refers to any income-producing real estate, whether existing or under development, including rental housing or real estate used by the owners of the property for conducting their business, purpose or activity, whether existing or under construction, that is not qualified as RRE property, and including social housing.*
>
> *(ESRB, 2019a, pp. 11–12)*

This definition of CRE excludes agricultural and forestry land, which is administered under separate, more elaborated data sets. As the Basel Committee on Banking Supervision (BCBS) argued, CRE exposure is secured by any immovable property that is not RRE as defined in paragraph 63 (Basel Committee on Banking Supervision [BCBS], 2017a, p. 23). CRE is primarily defined by exclusion criteria, as the term applies to all assets not defined as RRE, whose primary function is to provide space for humans to live. This definition was adapted in the CRR of the European Union (EU) (European Parliament Regulation 575/2023—CRR, 2013). While its simplicity might be appealing at first sight, like other definitions, it seemed rather inadequate for practical application. Addressing this challenge, the ESRB dedicated large parts of its 2015 report to the harmonisation of definitions, allowing for improved data comparability across the EU (ESRB, 2015). In 2019, the ESRB (2019b) further refined its initial definition of CRE as "commercial property including buildings [...] developed for the express purpose of providing income and/or a capital gain" (ESRB, 2015). Fig. 2.1 shows the variety of definitions of CRE provided by different supervisory bodies.

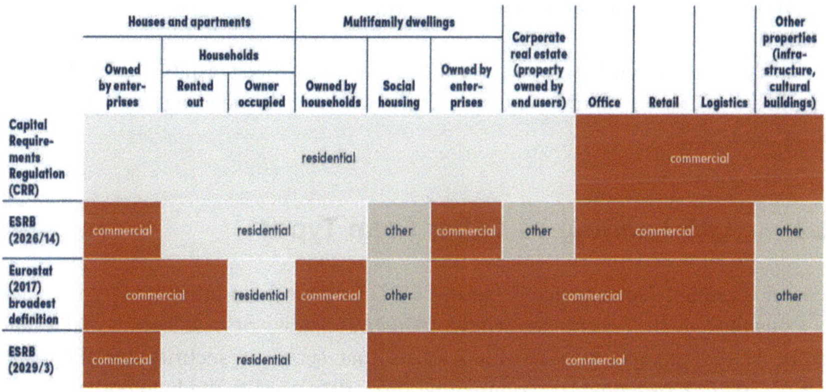

Fig. 2.1 Overview of CRE definitions. (Source: Redrawn from ESRB (2019a))

As shown, CRE assets were often assigned to various asset classes, including office, retail, commercial-residential, industrial/logistical, and others. Hospitality was either considered as a separate asset class or grouped under "other" (Office of the Comptroller of the Currency [OCC], 2022, p. 4). A key distinction was made between owner-occupied residential homes, and residential purpose properties let as a commercial activity, either by private property owners or by corporations. The segment of social housing was also an area of interest. In addition, all non-standard forms of land ownership, such as forestry, agricultural land, or land used for cultural or leisure activities, needed further classification.

According to the European Real Estate Association (EPRA), CRE in Europe accounted for approximately 7.7 trillion EUR at the end 2020, of which approximately 5.92 trillion EUR (6.71 trillion USD) stemmed from the 27 EU countries (EU-27), approximately 1.33 trillion EUR from the UK, and approximately 0.44 trillion EUR from the two non-EU countries Switzerland and Norway (EPRA, 2021, p. 7); no data was provided for the non-EU countries of former Yugoslavia and Iceland. The CRE sector accounted for about half of the GDP in both the EU and the UK (EPRA, 2021, p. 7). By way of comparison, the RRE stock in the EU-27 plus the UK was estimated to be worth approximately 24.9 trillion EUR in the previous year (EPRA/INREV, 2020, p. 4). According to INREV, the CRE industry employed around 4.2 million people and contributed 427 billion EUR to the European economy in 2021, representing approximately 2.8% of the GDP (EPRA/INREV, 2022, p. 2). According to EPRA's global comparative assessment, the estimated CRE value in all the 79 countries surveyed in its total markets table report was over 28.7 trillion EUR (32.4 trillion USD) at the end of 2020 (EPRA, 2021, p. 14).

While a basic understanding of CRE has now been established, attention should be focussed on the key characteristics of CRE lending, as opposed to other loan types.

2.2 CRE Lending vs Other Loan Types

One of the main features that separates CRE lending from other loan types, such as consumer loans, commercial and industrial loans, or residential real estate loans, is the linkage to real estate assets that serve as security for the loans (OCC, 2022). Consequently, commercial property serves as the loan collateral and primary source of loan repayments, generated by rental income or sale proceeds (Federal Reserve—OCC—FDIC, 2006). On the other hand, even if secured by mortgages on properties, corporate loans do not qualify as CRE loans in the narrow sense as their repayment is funded by the borrowers' operational business (OCC, 2022). To distinguish between different types of CRE loans, the joint statement of the key regulatory bodies of the United States of America (US) provided a classification (Federal Reserve—OCC—FDIC, 2006):

- loans for which cash flow from real estate is the primary source of repayment, in distinction from borrower loans, for which real estate collateral is taken as a secondary source of repayment or through an abundance of caution;
- land development and construction loans, including those for one-to-four-family residential mortgages and commercial construction loans;
- loans secured by multifamily residential property, as well as non-agricultural and non-residential property, for which the primary source of repayment is derived from rental income associated with the property, where at least 50 percent of the repayment comes from third-party rental income, or from the proceeds of the sale, refinancing, or permanent financing of the property; and
- loans to real estate investment trusts and unsecured loans to developers, provided that their performance is intricately linked to the performance of CRE markets.

Excluded from these categories are loans secured by non-farm or non-residential properties, where the primary source of repayment is cash flow from ongoing operations and activities conducted by the party or an affiliate of the party that owns the property.

In the following chapter, the CRE debt fund universe and its contextualisation in the alternative lending space are outlined.

2.3 Alternative Lending Space: The CRE Debt Fund Universe

In the alternative lending space, CRE debt funds generate returns primarily from interest, fees and loan repayments, while also providing the opportunity to benefit from increased valuations of commercial properties. Professional investors seem to expect the fairly stable returns and reasonable safety that are provided for by these threefold payments on commercial loans. Although investments in existing capital structures appear trustworthy at first sight, the risk remains that the expected payments on these loans cannot be met by borrowers. Typically, the sole or main security for the investments are the properties themselves, which can be subject to significant fluctuations in value.

Unlike banks, which manage deposits from private and business customers, debt funds are not subject to comparable strict regulations and public disclosure requirements. Many professional investors in debt funds are occupational pension funds and insurance companies, however, and these entities in turn manage the pension assets and insurance premiums of private and business customers. Even if the systemic risks to which insurance companies and pension funds are exposed are deemed to be lower than those facing banks, the residual risks for future pensioners and policyholders should be of concern. As this recognition has grown, insurance companies have increasingly been subject to the regulations of the European Insurance and Occupational Pensions Authority (EIOPA), most notably under the Solvency II Directive (2009/138/EC) (European Parliament Directive 2009/138 -Solvency II, 2006). However, these regulations have proved to be only partially or not at all relevant to many pension funds. Overall, the scope and level of detail of regulations for CRE loans applied by the European Securities and Markets Authority (ESMA) under the AIFMD (European Parliament Directive 2011/61-AIFMD I, 2011) are not comparable to those that apply to banks under the regulatory authority of the European Central Bank (ECB) and the national banking supervisors (i.e. Bundesanstalt für Finanzdienstleistungsaufsicht (BaFin)), as well as the European Banking Authority (EBA) (European Parliament Directive 2013/36—Capital Requirements Directive [CRD], 2013).

Together with national supervisory authorities, ESMA oversees the regulated market of the legal entities known as alternative investment fund managers (AIFMs), and listed about 3,000 active AIFMs in its database as of November

2023 (ESMA, 2023). This database distinguished between the various asset class focuses of alternative investment funds and issued a list including 2,480 CRE-related AIFMs, with a net asset value of 543 billion EUR. Regulated AIFMs often outsource portfolio management and origination to external companies, which are often the sponsors of debt fund vehicles, namely alternative investment funds (AIF). Disaggregated data on CRE debt funds cannot be found in the ESMA database.

To mitigate this shortfall, INREV regularly retrieves aggregated data on CRE debt funds which its members manage. The report from December 2023 included 117 fund vehicles managed by 40 investment managers with total target equity of 62.9 billion EUR and an average debt vehicle size of circa 530 million EUR (INREV, 2023a). According to this INREV survey, the number of vehicles had significantly risen from 50 in 2016 to 98 in 2022, and 117 in 2023 (INREV, 2023a). The vast majority (84% by target equity) of the total equity was concentrated in closed-end vehicles, with 65% (by target equity) being focussed on senior loan debt strategies. Over the last year of the period reviewed in the 2023 report, 19 newly launched vehicles were added, the largest increase since the debt universe was initiated in 2016. These 19 new fund vehicles increased the combined target equity by 2.6 billion EUR, representing a 19% increase by number and 4.3% by target equity from the overall INREV universe in 2022. Nine of these of 19 new vehicles followed a multi-country strategy, and six of the newly launched funds were open-ended vehicles. It is noteworthy that in October 2024, a new debt fund report by INREV (2024) was published, according to which the number of funds had increased to 123, and the target equity had risen from 62.9 billion EUR to 70 billion EUR. The majority of surveyed investors (61%) planned to increase their allocations in the CRE debt funds.

Another important source of information is the annually published Bayes CRE Lending Report, which highlights comparable data on CRE lending trends in the UK (Bayes Business School, 2023). When differentiating between EU-based and UK-based institutions, it should be borne in mind that lending activities are mostly multi-country and cross EU borders. The 2023 Bayes report covered a total of 81 lenders, of which 42 were banks and building societies, 26 were CRE debt funds, and 13 were insurance companies. According to this report, non-bank lending accounted for approximately 38% of the total, thereby setting a new record. In October 2024, the most recent UK CRE lending report by Bayes revealed that the share of alternative lenders (i.e. insurance companies and debt funds) of the surveyed CRE loan stock had even grown to 43% (Bayes Business School, 2024). An additional and noteworthy observation of the most recent Bayes report was the increased vulnerability of smaller institutions, which experienced higher loan-to-value (LTV) and lower interest cover ratio (ICR) than their larger peers (Bayes Business School, 2024).

Another publicly available source on CRE debt funds is Real Estate Capital's annual nominations of the so-called top 30 alternative CRE lenders (Real Estate Capital Europe, 2023, 2024), as well as the similar list of the so-called top 50 alternative lenders, published by Private Equity Real Estate (PERE, 2023).

As outlined earlier, debt funds are considered to be AIF in the EU, as opposed to regular investment funds of traded securities. In a predecessor form as so-called structured investment vehicles for collateralised debt obligation, alternative investment vehicles were considered to have contributed to the GFC. Following this financial crisis, the AIFMD I regulatory environment was introduced in 2011 through a directive of the AIFMD (ESMA -AIFMD reporting guideline, 2014; European Parliament Directive 2011/61-AIFMD I, 2011). This regulatory framework for managers of alternative investment vehicles included risk retention requirements of reporting to national regulatory bodies, such as the BaFin in Germany. The amended directive AIFMD II was adopted in November 2023 and entered into force in April 2024, with a transposition deadline of two years. AIFMD II clarified the ability of AIF to originate loans and tightened the regulatory framework governing managers of credit funds, so-called loan-originating AIF, and other funds originating loans, and also amended certain other rules applicable to all AIFMs (European Parliament, Directive 2024/927—AIFMD II, 2024; GrenbergTraurig, 2023). The new overarching loan requirements include inter alia:

- the requirement of retaining 5% of a loan for the first eight years of the loan's maturity;
- the restriction of limiting lending to other funds to no more than 20% of capital, and undertakings regarding collective investment in transferable securities funds and financial institutions;
- the obligation to disclose the full costs and expenses linked to the administration of the loans;
- the obligation to have full procedures and systems in place in relation to loan origination activities, and to review those procedures every year; and
- rules preventing funds from originating loans for the sole purpose of then transferring the exposure to third parties.

AIFMD II defined loan-originating AIFs as funds having an investment strategy to mainly act as loan originators, or as funds having originated loans which constitute at least 50% of their net asset value. Loan-originating AIFs are subject to detailed additional restrictions relating to leverage limits and risk management:

- leverage limits for open-ended funds, capped at 175%, and for closed-ended funds, capped at 300%; and
- risk management obligations, including the requirement to establish and implement effective policies, procedures and processes for loan origination.

In addition to the provisions specifically addressing loan-originating funds, AIFMD II introduced other notable changes relevant to the alternative investment industry. Of particular relevance for this study were the detailed new reporting requirements relating to the delegation of portfolio management and risk management functions.

The following section is dedicated to key concepts and technical terms, allowing for a better understanding of loan performance and loss minimisation.

2.4 Loan Performance and Loss Minimisation

With a certain degree of confidence, lenders expect that borrowers will repay loans, and that interest will be paid in addition to repayment of the principal sum. Even if lenders generally assume that their underwritten loans will be repaid, loan defaults do occur when subsequent events do not conform with initial business plans for the real estate. As will be argued, these expected credit losses (ECL) should be integrated into lenders' overall economic strategies, and should be accounted for in certain risk premiums of the interest margins.

At the same time, lenders are frequently faced with the dilemma that their returns are capped at the agreed interest level. Even if loans are effectively managed, lenders will not receive premiums or direct economic returns for effective loan risk management beyond the capped amounts. In contradistinction to equity investments, where the aim is usually to increase returns above the expected level, lenders are only able to optimise loan performance by minimising the potential for losses.

When loans default, unprepared lenders are in many cases no longer able to proactively drive processes, as time and capital scarcity might constrain attempts to deal with the issues arising. As it will be explored in this study, the issue might not be so much a lack of conviction about the need for effective loan risk management, as a reluctance to invest in non-revenue generating operations in advance. Even if such action does not primarily result in the maximisation of returns on individual loans, the secondary effects of effective loan risk management might occur, in particular the mitigation of payment default risk. The presumed effects of effective loan risk management should not be further dealt with from theoretical perspective at this point, however, as these form the centrepiece of the ex-ante propositions in Sect. 3.3, whose underlying hypotheses were tested in this research study.

2.5 Lender-Level Risk Management

In simple terms, the business model of a bank is to collect deposits from customers with a surplus of cash and to lend these to other customers in need of cash at a higher interest rate than that paid to depositors. This business model usually faces two key challenges: liquidity risks, and credit risks. Liquidity risks refer to a bank's inability to meet its obligations, as customers' bank deposits, if they are not fixed-term deposits, can be withdrawn at any time. Liquidity risks are usually created by the divergence in the terms of, on the one hand, assets, i.e. mid- to long-term loans, and, on the other, liabilities, i.e. short-term deposits. Credit risks refer to the possibility of losses occurring due to borrowers defaulting on their loans, and non-compliance with their contractual obligations.

As the focus of the study is predominately on closed-end debt funds and not banks, differences in risk profiles should be emphasised. It can generally be assumed that the greatest threats to debt funds' solvency are credit risks, not liquidity risks. As capital managers, CRE debt funds do not rely on customers' deposits, but on long-term investments of their professional investors. Another difference lies in the relative size structures of debt funds and banks, because the latter becoming insolvent can adversely affect the stability of the financial system and the real economy. These key differences between debt funds and banks, and how they influence risk management practices, will be discussed later in this section.

Risks categories for lenders were outlined by BaFin (2023) in its guidelines on minimal requirements for risk management by banks. In addition to the already discussed (i) liquidity risks; and (ii) credit risks; lender risks include (iii) market risks of losses on financial investments caused by adverse price movements, for instance changes in interest rates and equity or commodity prices, and foreign exchange fluctuations; and (iv) operational risks of losses caused by ineffective processes, policies and systems, including compliance risks. In the author's understanding, however, compliance risks should be listed as a separate category which should include not only illegal practices such as bribery and money laundering, but also risks relating to non-compliance with ESG regulations, as well as cyber risks and data protection risks, both of which could result in financial losses, the disruption of operations, and reputational damage. Theoretically, one could also interpret compliance risks as a cross-sectional category which is relevant to various pillars of a risk model. Interrelationships between risk groups should also be taken into account: for example, market risks often trigger credit risks. As will be discussed, different factors can have differing degrees of influence on risks, with differing consequences, as the extent to which operational and compliance risks can be controlled should naturally exceed that applicable to market risks. While not comprehensive, Fig. 2.2 provides an overview of the main risk categories and sub-categories.

As outlined in Fig. 2.3, risk management processes of lenders typically rely on three operational pillars: (i) business units (responsible for the development and implementation of strategies); (ii) compliance and risk management units (responsible for compliance monitoring and reporting on effectiveness of controls, and for the identification of risks and relevant mitigation measures); and (iii) internal and external audit units (responsible for reviewing accounting and financial and other operations, as well as for retrospective assurance of compliance with requirements). While the primary reporting line for internal audit units and compliance is usually the board of directors, risk management units frequently report to credit committees. These committees usually meet on a regular basis to consider applications for finance, to monitor the performance of existing credit portfolios, and to decide whether to amend or extend existing finance arrangements.

Risk category	Credit risk	Operational risk	Liquidity risk	Compliance risk	Market risk
Main risk	Default of counterparty	Ability to run the processes of a prudent lender	Outflow of short-term cash deposits	Laws and regulations	Changing market conditions
Sub risk	• Borrower quality • Sponsor quality • Financial structure • Legal structure • Asset-specific risk (not market risk) • Tenant quality	• Organisational processes • Decision process • Delegated authority • IT - risk • Outsourcing • Staffing (HR) • Training	• Short term liabilities vs. long-term/ illiquid assets • Access to diversified sources of capital • Availability of central bank lines • Mark to market valuations	• Legal risk • Anti-money laundering (AML) • Know your client (KYC) • Reputation • ESG • Cyber risk • Data protection	• Currency (FX) • Interest rate • Credit availability • GDP growth • Demand and supply of CRE • Legal and tax • Regulatory changes • Construction costs

Fig. 2.2 Risk management categories and sub-risks. (Source: own illustration (o. i.))

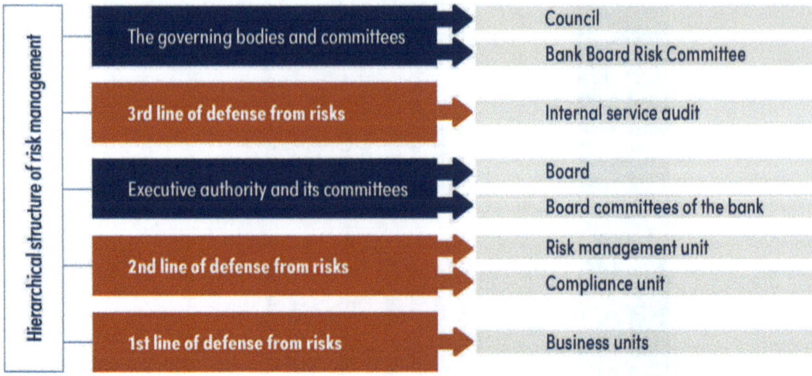

Fig. 2.3 Risk management defence lines. (Source: Redrawn from Prymostka & Prymostka (2019))

Risk management procedures and processes at banks in the EU are directed by the guidelines on risk management and accounting for ECL by the EBA (2017a) and the dated but still highly relevant principles for the management of credit risks by the BCBS (2000). Focussing on risk management in the narrow sense, the EBA defined the following key requirements: (i) management body and senior management responsibility; (ii) sound ECL methodologies; (iii) credit risks rating and grouping processes; (iv) adequacy of the allowance; (v) ECL model validation; (vi) experienced credit judgement; (vii) common processes, systems, tools and data; and (viii) disclosure. As almost timeless guideline, the BCBS (2000) identified not only factors leading to success, but also those that invite failure, including (i) the lack of thorough credit assessments; (ii) the lack of effective credit review processes; (iii) failure to monitor borrowers' or collateral values; (iv) failure to adequately assess the correlation between borrower creditworthiness and asset values in CRE lending; (v) subjective decision-making at senior management level; (vi) not taking sufficient account of business cycle effects in lending; and (vii) absence of a thoughtful consideration of downside scenarios and the so-called stress tests. More than twenty years after the BCBS guidelines were published, the ESRB field assessment of CRE risk practices in banks came to a sobering conclusion:

> *[For] most of the banks reviewed, the findings raise concerns about lending standards, collateral valuation, and monitoring processes. The examinations show that several banks have no underwriting criteria, do not monitor breaches of such criteria, or pay*

> *insufficient attention to cash flows, including in bad times. In general, banks have not sufficiently performed sensitivity analyses on CRE exposures, especially to measure the potential impact of an increase in interest rates. Because of these weaknesses, the affordability of some borrowers may not be as robust as banks had originally assumed. The examinations also identified basic shortcomings in collateral valuation, such as the failure to update appraisal reports in accordance with the CRR or to perform an ad hoc revaluation when market conditions changed. In addition, in many cases the valuation approach and the calibration of parameter values, such as the vacancy status of the property, the contractual rent, or the maintenance cost of the building, were not adequate, leading to significant asset value overstatement.*
>
> (ESRB, 2023, p. 4)

The ESRB's recent assessment of the current state of risk management practices at banks raised questions not just about regulatory impacts, but also about the limits of organisational transformation processes. The preceding ECB report (ECB, 2022) identified four key risk areas that needed to be kept under observation: (i) construction cost increases; (ii) interest rate normalisation, i.e., increases in rates and their impact on borrowers' ability to refinance; (iii) bifurcation of CRE into prime assets, which are fit for purpose and so-called ESG-ready, and non-prime assets, which are no longer fit for purpose and require repositioning; and (iv) climate transition and physical risks. In addition, four key areas requiring attention were identified: (i) loan origination; (ii) loan monitoring; (iii) accounting practices; and (iv) collateral value. Even though these assessments and derived recommendations were actually focussed exclusively on the banking sector, numerous key points that emerged from the analysis could equally be applied to the CRE debt fund sector. This transferability also applied to the categorisation of quantitative and qualitative approaches to risk monitoring. This view was again reiterated by the ECB in its recent Supervision Newsletter (2024a) in which it criticised banks' shortcomings in their dealings with CRE collateral and valuations in particular, including the definition of market value, marketing period, highest and best use, special assumptions, and the residual value method.

Literature dealing with the methods of CRE loan risk management was scarce, particularly with regard to the distinction between quantitative and qualitative approaches. Based on his own observations, the author has therefore endeavoured to fill this research gap (see Table 2.1).

Table 2.1 Qualitative vs. quantitative risk management activities at different loan stages.

Loan stage	Quantitative	Qualitative
Origination	• Analysis of property data • Market data (rents, sales, yields) • Stress testing of key parameters (sensitivity scenarios) • Expected credit loss	• Information covenants • Meetings • Semi-structured interviews • Site visits • Sponsor review of track record and solvency • Assessment of borrowers' risk monitoring processes • Market feedback • News search
Monitoring	• Borrower reporting • Cash flow • Market data (credit ratings, rents and yields) • Valuation report • Financial covenants • Other covenants • Stress testing of key parameters • Expected credit loss	• Information covenants • Quarterly meeting(s) with borrowers • Response analysis • Text-based analysis of borrower/ sponsor documents • Assessment of borrower-lender relationship • Assessment of borrowers' risk monitoring processes • Auditor feedback • Meeting with property managers • Meeting with brokers • Market feedback • News search

Source: o. i.

As in empirical social research, clear distinctions should be drawn between qualitative and quantitative methods, on the one hand, and between qualitative and quantitative data, on the other. This understanding implies that quantitative data might be fed into qualitative monitoring approaches. It is also important to note that both approaches can include manual and automated tasks.

Often based on, but not limited to personal interaction, qualitative loan risk monitoring and analysis tasks and instruments might include the following: (i) information covenants, such as written and oral progress reports; (ii) critical reviews of borrowers' risk management processes; (iii) continuous valuation of the quality and desirability of properties, including site visits and related meetings with borrowers, as well as with managers and tenants of properties; (iv) review of processes with auditors; (v) analysis of implicit potential (i.e., reputational guarantees by the sponsor or other parties); (vi) ongoing market research on borrowers, locations, and tenants; (vii) review of lease terms and conditions (e.g. option analysis from tenants' perspectives); (viii) frequent discussions with leasing and investment brokers, and potential investors; and (ix) obtaining feedback from other lenders, investors, brokers and valuers. Ideally, the result-oriented implementation of these tasks should be based on trustworthy relationships between different stakeholders that foster accountability and transparency. As will be argued, the instruments listed require a certain degree not just of professional experiences, but also of knowledge of human nature and the ability to read between the lines. As expert experiences will show, this can take a certain degree of courage and a thick skin, because those entrusted with monitoring tasks are not infrequently the bearers of bad news.

Qualitative information is understood as so-called soft data, which is difficult to measure precisely. Consequently, its interpretation requires contextual understanding and in-depth technical knowledge. As will be argued, soft and hard data should play distinct yet complementary roles in loan risk management. Hard data refers to measurable, verifiable and quantifiable information which is expressed numerically and can be analysed employing statistical methods. In the case of CRE debt funds, quantitative data typically refers to loan-level numerical analysis, which will be dealt with in more detail in the following chapter.

The limitations of quantitative analysis as an operational task of CRE debt funds should already be discussed at this point. Robust statistical interpretation of quantitative data requires a sufficient degree of standardisation and comparability. The Statistical Office of the European Union (Eurostat, 2017) and the ESRB (2015) have already criticised the lack of high quality market data on CRE, in contrast to the RRE space, which was characterised by higher levels of homogeneity and thus produced more comparable data.

At the end of this section, it is worth reiterating the initial argument about the differences in risk profiles between banks and debt funds. As argued, supervisory regulations for banks are much more stringent, which is due to the systemic risk potential given their larger size and their fiduciary role as deposit holders (EBA, 2017a, 2017b, 2018, 2020, 2021). Stricter supervision demands more rigorous risk management at portfolio level, and banks' larger staff sizes in principle allow them to set up appropriate specialised departments. As discussed, many debt funds are smaller in size and tend to focus their limited human resources on the management of individual loans. Conversely, however, the lower number of loans under management means that credit risks of individual loans could pose greater threats to the performance and solvency of debt funds. That said, it must be emphasised that debt funds are not a homogeneous group but vary considerably in size and structure (INREV, 2024). Any presumed relational connections between the funds' sizes and the effectiveness of their loan risk management should, however, not be further discussed at this point, as these are integral to the ex-ante propositions presented in Sect. 4.2, whose underlying hypotheses were tested in this research study.

In the next and final section of this chapter on key concepts and technical terms, the focus shifts from the organisational level of the lender to the operational level of CRE loans.

2.6 Loan-Level Risk Management

In the absence of literature on the topic of loan-level risk management in CRE debt funds, the following section is based primarily on the author's own observations. Firstly, the author argues that in the case of CRE debt funds, the widely used terms "portfolio management" or "asset management" should be replaced with the term "loan risk management". The motivation for this is that in widespread practice, there is a factual distinction between portfolio management in the narrower and the broader senses. In the narrower sense, portfolio management implies that covariance risks should be kept to a minimum by maintaining balanced and diversified loan portfolios. This narrower sense of portfolio management is primarily practised by banks, which often simultaneously manage hundreds if not thousands of loans. In contrast, CRE debt funds generally manage much smaller portfolios of, say, ten to one hundred loans, which might differ in terms of asset class, risk profile, and stage of development, but which are in most cases administratively managed at the individual loan level. For this reason, a further risk category should be added to the lender-level risk management risks mentioned in the previous subchapter: concentration risks. Two types of concentration risk have been identified by Philipps (2021): (i) name concentration risks, which might be caused by the uneven distribution of loan exposure to individual borrowers; and (ii) sectoral concentration risks, which might arise from the uneven distribution of exposure to particular sectors, regions, industries or products. This study will analyse whether the observed focus of CRE debt funds on individual loans might have led to proverbial failures of not being able to see the forest for all the trees, or, in other words, to neglect of the overall trend of macroeconomic developments.

The author's observations suggest that the management of loans can generally be categorised as (i) administrative tasks without credit decisions; (ii) standard management tasks with standard credit decisions; and (iii) non-standard management tasks, i.e. special decisions concerning credit or restructuring issues (see Fig. 2.4).

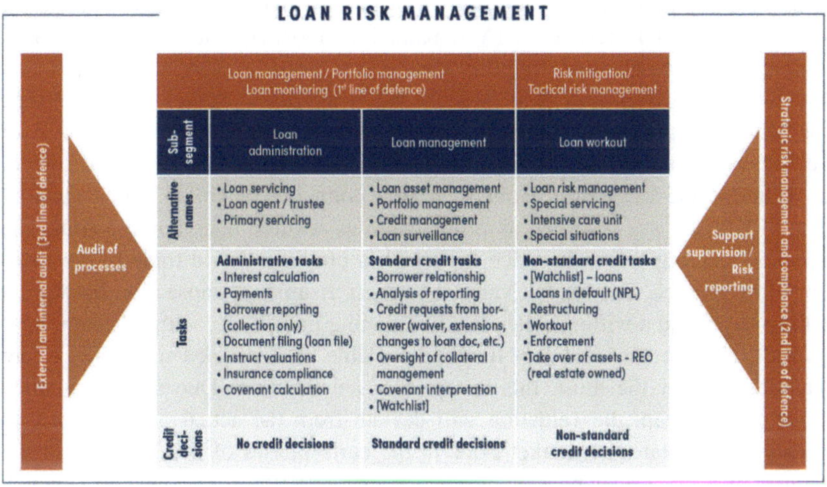

Fig. 2.4 Loan risk management tasks and nomenclature. (Source: o. i.)

Loan-level risk management primarily concerns credit risks and market risks due to the causal effects that may arise. As such, the detection of sub-performing loans (SPLs) or non-performing loans (NPLs) and the identification and reassessment of measures that were deemed suitable to mitigate the consequences of loan default should be core tasks. This should involve monitoring and, if necessary, reassessing the risks already identified during underwriting, adding risks identified post-closing, and determining the effectiveness of previously identified and implemented mitigation measures. In this regard, relevant tasks should include (i) classification of risks; (ii) stress testing and scenario analysis; (iii) watchlist analysis; (iv) calculation of expected and unexpected losses; (v) workout of defaulted positions; and (vi) enforcement and management of assets effectively under lender control. In addition, loan-level risk management should also include (vii) the supervision of risk management processes under the purview of borrowers or service providers; (viii) sharing of lessons learnt and key factors of success and failure with origination and underwriting teams; and (ix) reporting to supervisors and at credit committees. In practice, it was found that it could not automatically be assumed that all these functions were bundled in one administrative unit. The extent to which CRE debt funds were able to fulfil these tasks effectively forms the centrepiece of this research study.

Several key performance indicators (KPIs) exist that aid managers in assessing loan quality. Of these, the LTV remained the most commonly used indicator, although concerns about its viability have been voiced by professionals and academics alike (Grovenstein et al., 2005; Ono et al., 2021; Stokes & Cox, 2022). The LTV is commonly calculated based on the outstanding loan amount over the last valuation. While the loan amount as such remained rather undisputed, the value of the asset turned out to be the point of contention. The valuation of a CRE asset was regarded as problematic as it often does not constitute the so-called clearing price, the price for which a property would trade in the then-prevailing market. The market value, however, assumes a transaction between a willing buyer and a willing seller in a functioning market, i.e. with sufficient buyers and sellers present and debt funding available. In distressed situations, where valuations matter the most, this is typically not the case. Due to the so-called valuation time gap, the valuation will deviate from the actual market price, as it tends to overstate the market price in the early phases of a developing crisis. Maintenance costs that became necessary in the medium to long term, which were often overlooked, should also be considered.

Other frequently used KPIs refer to interest service coverage and debt service coverage. For the ICR, the net operating income of the asset is divided by the interest. For the debt service cover ratio (DSCR), the net operating income is divided by the sum of interest and amortisation. Both, ICR and DSCR work from backward- and forward-looking perspectives. Debt yield constitutes the link between the abovementioned KPIs. Dividing net operating income over the loan amount and calculating a quasi-asset yield for the loan amount links net operating income to the debt amount outstanding. This procedure provides the decision-making basis for which yield (or cap rate, in more common US parlance) the asset would need to trade for the loan to be repaid. Consequently, the debt yield circumvents the problems associated with property valuations.

In the absence of existing KPIs for effective loan risk management, the author identified a range of potential operational indicators, including (i) the number of persons employed for the management of performing loans (PLs), SPLs and NPLs; (ii) the percentage distribution between PLs, SPLs and NPLs; (iii) the number of SPLs and NPLs to be managed by the risk management unit; (iv) the number of loans (currently) in the restructuring process; (v) the average time required for the production of reports and credit memoranda; (vi) the number of meetings with borrowers per year; (vii) the average time taken for incident reporting; (viii) the average time from the date a default is recognised until the first restructuring dialogue over a loan takes place with the borrower; (ix) the average time from the dialogue taking place to resolution or enforcement; and (x) recovery ratios.

In addition to determining these quantitative process indicators, the author will argue that often overlooked so-called soft factors should also be considered, such as (i) clear separation of roles and responsibilities between origination and loan management, including communication with borrowers and servicers; (ii) unambiguous internal reporting and communication lines, with direct reporting obligations of loan risk managers to the board of directors; (iii) recognition of the qualifications required for loan risk management, considering the need for both analytical and negotiation skills; (iv) conviction of the worth of a resource-intensive operating unit that at first glance does not generate income; (v) recognition of risk managers through appropriate renumeration and staffing of the unit commensurate with the workload; and (vi) efficiency gains through state-of-the-art information technology.

The aforementioned sizes and personnel resources of CRE debt funds should be considered, as expenses for loan risk management must be factored in. The costs of maintaining a loan risk management unit must naturally be reasonable in relation to the number of loans managed, through which these administrative costs must be met. In order to save on personnel costs, including ancillary costs, outsourcing certain tasks to external service providers remains an option. As will be argued, however, the reins should not be too loose, as effective loan risk monitoring should be in the lender's own interest. A principle already described in the early work of Akerlof (1970) is that bad loan management practices, driven by the desire for quick gains at the expense of anticipatory action, may replace good management practices, in the same way that bad money may replace good money. The environment of the alternative lending space, where competition between debt funds for the acquisition of new loans was high and margins were consequently low, must be considered in this analysis. In addition to this contextualisation, the author will argue that CRE debt funds faced further challenges in the implementation of effective loan risk management, such as (i) the limited availability of specific qualifications and required skill sets needed for risk management, which were often only found among highly experienced professionals; (ii) so-called disaster myopia, defined as the cognitive dissonance of ignoring risks that appeared less likely than they actually were, in particular in the upcycle when values rose, unemployment was low, and demand for CRE was high; and (iii) discomfort in the presence of a critical credit management team that frequently raised objections at credit decision meetings (the desire not to have to deal with unpleasant business). The extent to which these challenges materialised in reality is an integral part of this analytical study.

Following this provision of a basic understanding of key concepts and technical terms, the next chapter provides a thorough discussion of the current state of research, including not only peer-reviewed academic writings, as discussed above in the author's earlier literature review synopsis, but also relevant sources beyond the peer-reviewed academic sphere.

Current State of Research 3

The research questions to be presented in this chapter were logically derived from the gaps identified in existing academic research. Research gaps are unanswered questions or unresolved problems which reflect a current lack of knowledge in that space. Most of the available academic literature focussed on bank-specific variables of loan underwriting, including initial credit risk assessments, and the lender-borrower relationship. Loan-specific aspects remained clearly under-researched, as did credit and disaggregated loan facets. Not even a third of the academic papers that were surveyed focussed on CRE or, more specifically, on CRE banking loans or secured credit, while the overwhelming majority of studies were connected to RRE, small and medium-sized enterprises, agricultural land, corporates, and management buyout as main loan collateral types. Of the CRE-specific studies, most analysed data from the US, and only a few used data from Europe. The alternative lending space remained virtually untouched by academic research. Consequently, the same applied to the loan-level risk management of debt funds.

The following accounts are summaries of a more detailed literature review synopsis, which the author submitted to SDA Bocconi in September 2022 (Hammel, 2022). For submission of the thesis, this chapter was not thoroughly updated by the inclusion of peer-reviewed academic research published since submission of the initial literature review synopsis (2023–2024). The reason for this was that the state of academic knowledge current at the time had initially informed the definition of the research objectives and the formulation of the research questions. Nevertheless, the author took more current publications into account during the analytical process. A complete updating of the review of the academic literature review synopsis would, however, have distorted the logical sequence of the analytical process, since this was based on the initial review.

W. Hammel, *Loan Risk Management of Commercial Real Estate Debt Funds*,
https://doi.org/10.1007/978-3-658-48912-0_3

3.1 Structured Methodology: Peer-Reviewed Academic Research

The subject under investigation, CRE loan risk management, had not yet been conceptually defined, and therefore did not appear as a key theme in academic and popular literature searches. An initial search within the two major databases, Web of Science (WoS) and Scopus, showed a strong funnelling effect for CRE from the wider research field, suggesting that the clear majority of academic work had been done on RRE. Combining the search string "real estate" with "commercial" as a preface, thereby suggesting that "commercial real estate" might be a standing fixed term that would be used in abstracts or titles, led to a reduction of the findings from over 30,000 to below 1,000. Once the word sequence was combined with the term "loan", the search results were reduced to below 100. Adding the term "manage" yielded only six and 12 records in WoS and Scopus, respectively. From the results of these search strings, it was concluded that the concept under review was deemed to be of only limited relevance in the academic debate current at the time. Therefore, a wider search algorithm was employed to allow more related literature to be included.

For initial information retrieval, only English-language peer-reviewed journal articles ranked by the Chartered Association of Business Schools, the Academic Journal Guide, and the École Supérieure des Sciences Economiques et Commerciale's Ranking of Journals (both 2021 versions), were included. The earliest results from the search were from 1994 for WoS, and 1995 for Scopus. As the databases applied different content and search methodologies, each with its own strengths and weaknesses, it was assumed that triangulation of these databases would be the best practice, despite the practical problems that this approach obviously entailed (Caputo & Kargina, 2022; Caputo et al., 2021; Echchakoui, 2020). Applying journal rating criteria (i.e. only peer-reviewed rated journals) and line-by-line examination of full references, 40 articles in 34 rated journals out of total 168 initial suggestions remained in the WoS database search (search date: 24 August 2022). The results of the Scopus search yielded 44 articles (out of initially 240 records) in 38 rated journals (search date: 6 September 2022). Out of the combined 84 articles, 31 were double entries that appeared in both searches, hence, the total number was reduced to 53 articles in 43 journals. To detect possible limitations in the data bases and, thus, to prevent the search results from being incomplete, the snowball backward search suggested by Webster & Watson (2002) was applied. For the forward search, only the Scopus database was used, as it contained the larger set of documents. Together, the backward and forward searches added 11 records to the initial 53 records, hence, a total number of 64 documents from 52 peer reviewed and ranked journals were used for this review.

Descriptive analysis allowed the interpretation of a timeline of sampled publications, of which more than a third (38%) stemmed from the latest time quantile, notably the period 2017–2022. While the small sample size was unlikely to provide statistical relevance, the findings revealed the cyclical movement of academic interest in debt and its role in financial crises. Regulatory bodies published a significant amount of data post-GFC, which was used for analytical interpretation. Although just a fraction (9%) of articles were pre-millennial, interestingly, these were among the highest rated and most widely cited references in the entire sample. Furthermore, the publication count by journal ratings revealed that Real Estate Economics and the Journal of Real Estate Literature together accounted for 11% of all sampled studies. However, none of the articles published in these two journals ranked among the top ten of most widely cited references in the sample.

Finally, bibliometric analysis for the statistical interpretation of text-based information was applied to gather bibliographic information about the scientific literature. For the analysis of the bibliographic information, bibliometric software such as VOSviewer (van Eck & Waltman, 2011) and Bibliometrix, based on R statistical software (Aria & Cuccurullo, 2017), was utilised for this literature review. The bibliometric analysis yielded broad categorical results, which were graphically illustrated in the authors' detailed literature review synopsis (Hammel, 2022).

In the following sections, the review of peer-reviewed academic literature is structured in accordance with the identified concepts, under which each reference was synthesised as suggested by Webster and Watson (2002). Following Manz (2019a), as a first step, each reference was categorised with 35 applicable descriptive first-order labels. Secondly, condensed labels for ten broader categories, also referred to as axial- or second-order codes, were applied (J. Corbin & Strauss, 1990). Thirdly, based on these categories, a concept-centric framework was presented that acknowledged three aggregated dimensions, namely macroeconomic, lender-specific, and loan-specific considerations.

In the absence of wider scientific research on the subject under review, relevant sources beyond peer-reviewed academic literature proved to be of particular interest for the desk study and are presented in the final section of this chapter.

3.2 Macroeconomic Considerations

Banking crises and economic cycles are considered as reoccurring and integral parts of economic life (BIS, 2004; Davis & Zhu, 2011; Herring & Wachter, 1998; Reinhart & Rogoff, 2009; Wheaton, 1999). While the effects of such economic cycles on CRE seemed to be fairly undisputed, these cause-and-effect relationships were surprisingly not given the attention they deserve in academic writing.

Firstly, CRE-specific studies were reviewed. Referencing data retrieved from more than 200 European banks during the period 2001– 2012, Baselga-Pascual et al. (2015) confirmed that the risks to which banks were exposed were inversely related to their capitalisation, profitability, efficiency, and liquidity. Bassett & Marsh (2017) thematised the effects of pre-GFC regulations of the Federal Register of US banks, published in 2006 with the aim of reducing bank exposure to CRE loans. According to the study, the macroprudential guidance provided by the Federal Reserve Board ("the Fed") resulted in a reduction in the percentage share of CRE lending. It is particularly noteworthy that the Fed at the time focussed on the CRE lending space, to the detriment of the housing market that ultimately caused the GFC, as housing debt was largely securitised and, hence, not included in the banks' balance sheets. Ben Jabra et al. (2017) examined the relationship between the determinants of risk tolerance in the European banking sector during major financial crises, namely bank risks, bank characteristics, and regulatory, institutional and macroeconomic variables. Using a sample of 280 banks from 26 European countries, the study showed that bank capitalisation and bank size had negative impacts on insolvency risks during the period 2005–2015. According to these findings, higher competition negatively affected risk tolerance, while macroeconomic variables such as inflation had an effect on NPL ratios. In his early analysis, Shanker (1994) focussed on legal aspects, in particular lenders' risks of exposure to environmental liability, as stipulated under the (new at the time) US legislation. Environmental matters were not a widely discussed field in later academic writings, apart from Mathew et al. (2021) and An and Pivo (2020). However, an increase in significance is certainly to be expected in view of the growing relevance of ESG-related compliance risks.

Secondly, non-CRE-specific studies were reviewed. Demyanyk and Hasan (2010) provided an overview of methodologies applied for the prediction and explanation of the underlying systemic and structural problems that led to the GFC. Akin et al. (2020) identified one of the main causes and stated that insider trades anticipated the poor performance of the relevant banks. Modina & Pietrovito (2014) surveyed more than 9,000 Italian small and medium-sized enterprises during the period under review (2006–2010), confirming their hypothesis that the capital structures of companies were strong predictors for default risks. By focusing on the time period 1970–2005, Deakin et al. (2017) provided a pre-GFC study, examining the impact of creditor rights on credit availability. The literature review on this topic led to the conclusion that civil law countries, such as France and Germany, had an elevated level of protection from creditors in the form of control over the management of debtor firms. Common law countries, in particular the US and the UK, exhibited a higher degree of protection in relation to rights over firm assets. This in turn led to the conclusion that laws strengthening creditors' control over debtor firms had positive effects on the expansion of private credit, while reforms increasing secured creditors' rights had negative effects in this regard.

3.3 Lender-Specific Considerations

Peer-reviewed academic literature on lender-level risk management, as defined in Sect. 2.5, was scarce. The few available publications focussed on bank-specific variables of loan underwriting, including initial credit risk assessments, and the lender-borrower relationship. Loan-specific management aspects remained clearly underrepresented. Published academic work on the borrower-lender relationship was thus of particular importance for the loan management focus of this thesis.

Interesting aspects of the lender-borrower relationship included the imbalance of access to information between the borrower, whose main focus of economic activity was the specific loan, and the lender, who was simultaneously dealing with a multitude of borrowers. Academic research focussed on which characteristics made good relationships between borrowers and lenders, and how these relationships influenced behaviour (Harding & Sirmans, 2002; Riddiough & Wyatt, 1994). For example, it was discussed how certain behaviours of borrowers could influence lenders' responses, such as willingness to extend or enforce mortgages, or offer discounted pay offs. As Uzzi & Gillespie (2002) argued, good and trustworthy relationships should benefit both sides. In this understanding, the borrower should benefit from obtaining favourable credit terms, while the lender should overcome the information asymmetry and would be enabled to embark on more collaborative solutions in the event of default.

The academic debate was silent on the question of what prerequisites must be met for outsourcing loan management activities to service providers as intermediaries between lenders and borrowers. There was also no academic literature on qualifications and experiences needed for effective loan management.

3.4 Loan-Specific Considerations

Some academic writing deals with loan portfolio management in the banking sector, although, as explained in Sect. 2.6, the conceptual distinction between portfolio management and loan management was not clearcut. The fact that peer-reviewed academic publications were silent on the subject of loan-by-loan risk management in the alternative lending space had consequences for the desk study's source research. As already mentioned, in the absence of wider scientific research, the author had to resort to sources beyond peer-reviewed academic literature on the subject under review.

One of the foremost reasons for these research gaps seemed to be economists' preference for quantitative analysis based on hard data, which was not publicly available in the alternative lending space. The author speculates that, in the near future, the focus of academic research might gradually move towards the topic of loan-by-loan risk management. This speculation is based on the increasing relevance of compliance risks, in particular with regard to ESG requirements, in accordance with the EU rules for sustainable finance under the new EU taxonomy (European Parliament Regulation 2020/852—EU Taxonomy, 2020; European Parliament—Directive 2021/2167 on credit servicers and credit purchasers, 2021/ 24.11.2021). While CRE lenders might not be able to influence the ESG performance of assets, they could direct their lending efforts to ESG-accredited projects, which might be easier to finance under better credit terms. Against this background, it is likely that regulatory authorities might demand the publication of loan-by-loan data, in order to make compliance with the ESG requirements verifiable. As argued, the associated provision of hard data could arouse more interest on the part of economic scholars involved in quantitative analyses.

3.5 Relevant Sources Beyond Peer-Reviewed Academic Literature

Relevant sources beyond peer-reviewed academic literature included (i) publications of national and supranational banking regulators and supervisors; (ii) reference books, textbooks, guidelines and glossaries, including those in the field of law; and (iii) unpublished academic writings and non-academic research reports.

Among the supranational banking regulators and supervisors, which provided numerous publications of central relevance to this study, were (i) the ECB as the central bank of EU countries and supervisor of all systemic banks in the eurozone; (ii) the EBA as an independent authority playing a key role in safeguarding the integrity and robustness of the EU banking sector to support financial stability; (iii) the ESRB, which was established to oversee the financial system of the EU and to mitigate and prevent systemic risk; and (iv) ESMA, whose mission is to improve investor protection and promote stable, regulated financial markets. Relevant national banking regulators and supervisors include (i) BaFin, the German federal institution which supervises banks, financial service institutions, and insurance undertakings and is itself supervised by the Federal Ministry of Finance; and (ii) the Prudential Regulation Authority, the UK financial services regulatory body which is responsible for the prudential regulation and supervision of banks, building societies, credit unions, insurers, and major investment firms.

Recent publications by these bodies most relevant to this research study include (i) *Commercial real estate: connecting the dots* (ECB, 2022, 2024c); (ii) *Guidance to banks on non-performing loans* (ECB, 2017, 2018); (iii) *Guidelines on loan origination and monitoring* (EBA, 2020); (iv) *Guidelines on credit institutions' credit risk management practices and accounting for expected credit losses* (EBA, 2017a); (v) *Vulnerabilities in the EEA commercial real estate sector* (ESRB, 2023); (vi) *Methodologies for the assessment of real estate vulnerabilities and macroprudential policies: commercial real estate* (ESRB, 2019a); (vii) *Report on vulnerabilities in the EU commercial real estate sector* (ESRB, 2018); and (viii) AIFMD I and II (European Parliament Directive 2011/61-AIFMD I, 2011; European Parliament, Directive 2024/927—AIFMD II, 2024). The German federal financial markets regulator BaFin published its guidelines on minimal requirements for risk management by banks (BaFin, 2023), while the only major related publication on CRE by the Bank of England is *Commercial property and financial stability* (Bank of England, 2013). While the UK is technically a third-party country from an EU perspective and is no longer directly bound by European directives, it must be borne in mind that all rules introduced into national law before the end of December 2020 remain in force till amended or replaced. The consecutive capital adequacy regulations published by the BCBS (2015, 2017a, 2019, 2021a, 2021b) apply to the banking industries in EU countries and the UK. The publications *Principles for the management of credit risks*, *Principles for operational resilience*, and *Revisions to the principles for the sound management of operational risk* (BCBS, 2000, 2021a, 2021b), respectively, should also be highlighted in this regard. A recent study by the International Monetary Fund (IMF) investigated the impact of CRE on financial stability in Germany (IMF, 2024), complementing an earlier study on the dynamics of NPL in banking crises (IMF, 2019).

Even if they did not directly relate to the geographical focus of this research study, the publications of US regulators and supervisors were of more general interest. These included (i) the Federal Reserve, as the central banking system; (ii) the FDIC, an independent agency created by the US Congress to maintain stability and public confidence in the nation's financial system; and (iii) the OCC as an independent bureau within the US Department of the Treasury that serves to charter, regulate, and supervise all national banks, thrift institutions, and the federally licensed branches and agencies of foreign banks. Relevant key publications included (i) *Statement on prudent risk management for commercial real estate lending* (Federal Reserve—OCC—FDIC, 2012); (ii) *Interagency guidelines for real estate lending policies* (Federal Reserve, 2021), (iii) *Concentrations in commercial real estate lending, sound risk management practices* (Federal Reserve—OCC—FDIC, 2006); and (iv) *Commercial real estate lending* (OCC, 2022).

Various reference books and textbooks on CRE investments cover debt as a subordinate theme (Brown, 2005; Geltner, 2007; Goddard & Marcum, 2012). Morri and Mazza (2015), Brueggemann & Fisher (2019), Isaac (2020), and Lauer (2021) are dedicated to CRE debt in Europe in noteworthy detail. Unfortunately only available as a German language publication, Lauer (2021) provided a remarkable textbook covering the entire CRE lending process, including risk management and workouts. Available in both English and German language versions, a comprehensive glossary of CRE lending terms and terminology was provided by Trübestein and Pruegel (2013). Covering the subject from a more practice-orientated viewpoint and aiming at US private investors as audience, the textbook of the Mortgage Bankers Association of America (2002) should not go unmentioned. Earlier writings on the subject of mortgage lending were provided by Bryant (1962) and by Dasso and Khun (1983). Both the history and the current state of the alternative lending space and its regulatory settings in Europe were investigated by Peridis (2022).

A wide array of legal literature was available on CRE property law, published in both academic journals and grey literature formats, with the latter category mostly being on corporate webpages by law firms as briefing notes for clients. Noteworthy was the electronic library of the Verband Deutscher Pfandbriefbanken

(VDP), which represents the interests of the Pfandbrief (mortgage) banks in Germany. The VDP electronic library includes not only more than fifty publications on specific aspects of mortgage-related legal matters in various European jurisdictions, but also a variety of market reports. The guidelines and templates of the UK Loan Market Association (2024) were an important additional resource dealing with the European CRE lending space. As a German language version, an annotated CRE loan agreement was recently provided by Gumpp (2021). The contexts of economic crises also encouraged various textbooks on CRE loan defaults and NPL workouts, such as Robert Morris Associates (1984), Saft (1991), Rottke & Gentgen (2008), Dick (2010) and Köchling & Schalast (2017), and more recently Manz (2019b) and Scardovi and Bezzecchi (2019). The European Association for Investors in Non-Listed Real Estate Vehicles regularly publishes reports on European Real Estate debt (INREV, 2023b, 2024) and the debt fund universe of its members (INREV, 2022, 2023a, 2024). The frequently cited key study on the economic business model of CRE lenders by McKinsey (2009) identified CRE lending as a high risk activity with severe agency problems. This was further underscored by the reports of the UK Property Industry Alliance Debt Group (2017, 2018), together with its peer, the UK Investment Property Forum (Investment Property Forum [IPF], 2014, 2017), which made multiple recommendations for the improvement of CRE lending frameworks. Furthermore, an analysis of defaulted loans from the GFC era was recently published by the research team of the Bank of America (2024).

The recently completed bachelor's degree thesis on alternative financing of commercial property by debt funds and insurance companies by Hinkel (2024), which was limited to web-based research, should be given special mention, as it served as a cornerstone database for the author's survey design.

The following chapter will present the research questions, as they were derived from the research gaps identified as key findings of the academic literature review. Verifiable ex-ante propositions, providing the author's predictions of the research outcomes, are presented. Interrelations between concepts are outlined, forming the building blocks of the suggested theoretical impact model.

4 Research Questions and Ex-Ante Propositions

A grounded theory implies a theoretical model of mechanisms and processes that is grounded in reality (J. M. Corbin & Strauss, 2015; Merriam & Tisdell, 2016). While this methodological approach to qualitative research will be elaborated on in the following chapter on research design and methodology, the first steps of grounded theory analysis should already be introduced in this chapter on research questions and ex-ante propositions. The first stage of developing a grounded theory served the development of concepts, and was based on the mining of data from documents, and from systematic observation. This delivered the building blocks of the theory that would be tested and verified by conducting semi-structured expert interviews (Charmaz, 2014; J. Corbin & Strauss, 1990). The overarching goal was to identify causal mechanisms that shed light on the relationship between practices of risk management and loan performance, thereby considering other intervening factors. The qualitative design was, however, emergent and flexible, and therefore responsive to changes in conditions of the study process. Accordingly, in order to formulate the final set of research hypotheses to be tested and verified, the author reviewed the preliminary research questions, tentative ex-ante propositions, and derived assessment dimensions and categories outlined in the initial research proposal (Hammel, 2023).

4.1 Research Questions

The central research question flowed from the purpose statement and reflected the author's thinking on the most significant factors of the study. Responding to this research question should contribute to closing the identified gaps in research, subject to restrictions imposed by current data limitations. In essence, this study explored the causal mechanisms underlying decisions and actions taken by the

W. Hammel, *Loan Risk Management of Commercial Real Estate Debt Funds*,
https://doi.org/10.1007/978-3-658-48912-0_4

stakeholders concerned. The research interest derived from the theoretical framework, and took into consideration (i) stakeholders' interests, relations, preferences and perceptions; (ii) their actions, and the intended and unintended effects of such actions; and (iii) external influencing factors. The central research question assumed the existence of a causal mechanism between loan risk management practices (the cause) and loan performance (the effect). It should be explicitly emphasised that the assumption was not one of mono-causality, but of multi-causality, taking alternative explanations for observable events and phenomena into consideration. Accordingly, the two-staged central research question was formulated as follows:

- What were the loan risk management practices of CRE debt funds, and what were the plausible effects of these practices on loan performance?

As sub-topics of this central theme, specific sub-questions were formulated. Sub-questions were identified along assessment dimensions which served to frame the ex-ante propositions which will be introduced in the following section. These sub-questions were formulated as follows:

- To what extent did corporate structures of debt funds create favourable or unfavourable conditions for effective loan risk management?
- How were loan risk management units anchored in the corporate structures of debt funds?
- How was loan risk management integrated in the corporate processes of debt funds?
- Did corporate cultures determine attitudes and behaviours towards risk monitoring, and if so, in what way?
- What were the key characteristics of the relationships between lenders, borrowers and service providers, and did these characteristics determine the effectiveness of loan risk management?
- What qualitative and quantitative loan risk monitoring practices could be observed in the units responsible for managing CRE debt funds?
- What were the key factors accounting for the success of effective loan risk management?
- Did external factors such as market cycles and the corporate environment influence loan performance, and if so, how were these interrelated with debt funds' loan risk management?

– Did these contextual factors influence both risk behaviour and loan risk monitoring practices of debt funds, and if so, in what way?

By and large, the higher-level questions of how loan performance of debt funds impacted the wider CRE lending environment and, in the next logical step, the economy, lay beyond the defined scope of the research study. Providing robust and reliable information to respond to these questions would have required not only a wider range of referenceable academic writing on this thematic area, but first and foremost access to statistically representative data. Due to their significance, these overarching questions were, nevertheless, kept in mind during the analytical research process, and perception-based expert responses on potential macroeconomic impacts of debt funds' loan performance were presented. While not directly referencing the central research question, this brief excursus fitted logically into the overall context and should add value to the scientific outcome of the thesis.

4.2 Ex-Ante Propositions and Theoretical Models

To deliver predictions about the research outcomes, ex-ante propositions were formulated. Evidence gathered during the data collection process served to test and verify the ex-ante propositions that had been made. These propositions related to the analytical sub-questions presented in Sect. 4.1, thereby, narrowing and dismantling predictions to be made for the overarching research question, and mitigating the complexity of the causal mechanisms to be tested.

The rationale for the formulation of the ex-ante propositions was based on the literature review, systematic observations, and several exploratory discussions with representatives of the Department of Land Economy at the University of Cambridge (UK) and the Commercial Real Estate Finance Council, and with heads and senior members of selected debt funds. These exploratory discussions were not recorded or transcribed, as they were intended solely to identify themes and potential strategies for the research design. The author made use of pre-defined categories and assessment dimensions to formulate the following ex-ante propositions:

I. The company size of debt funds, particularly during their growth phases with limited financial and personnel resources, posed administrative and operational challenges to loan risk management, and limited portfolios provided little headroom for balancing off loan-by-loan losses.
II. As the main focus of debt funds was predominantly on profit maximisation rather than on loss minimisation, resource-intensive but non-revenue generating loan risk management units were often ignored.
III. Due to so-called disaster myopia, defined as the cognitive dissonance of ignoring risks that seem less likely than they actually are, especially during economic upswings with rising property values, debt funds often understood risk management primarily as credit risk assessment at loan underwriting, and to a lesser degree as an ongoing management task.
IV. In relation to borrowers, lenders were exposed to an information asymmetry which needed to be overcome in order for them to embark on more timely and collaborative solutions in the event of loan default.
V. The receipt of non-standardised reports (which could therefore not be meaningfully compared) from borrowers and servicers, which had to be processed by loan risk management units in time-consuming work processes, led to reduced efficiency, while personal interaction between borrowers, lenders and servicers remained restricted to the minimum.
VI. The units responsible for loan risk management often used outdated information technologies, requiring more time for the completion of tasks and thereby leading to inefficiency in workflows.
VII. As debt funds were not subject to strict regulatory supervision and publicity requirements, they often exposed themselves to increased levels of credit risk due to the higher allocation of riskier loans, as they tended to invest in asset classes, regions and capital structures from which traditional financial institutes had withdrawn.
VIII. Against the backdrop of the green transition, debt funds increasingly directed their lending efforts towards ESG-accredited projects, with the aim of avoiding compliance risks that might turn into loan-level risks.
IX. In contrast to the portfolio management practices of banks, the loan-by-loan risk monitoring of many debt funds exposed them to higher concentration risks.

X. Success factors of efficient loan risk management included the recognition of personnel resources and required qualifications; high quality loan underwriting; efficiency gains through state-of-the-art information technology; standardisation of reporting by borrowers and servicers; clear reporting and communication lines; and the timely implementation of mitigation measures for credit risks, which depended on trustworthy collaboration between the stakeholders.

XI. Even if primary effects such as an increase in maximum returns of individual loans would not materialise through effective loan risk management, the early mitigation of borrowers' payment defaults should result in the secondary effect of minimising potential losses.

XII. Notwithstanding multicausality, there were contextual factors that could be assumed to have had particular influence on loan performance; market risks were precisely what should have been monitored, as their potential to cause credit risks should have been evaluated, and the likelihood of their being influenced by mitigation measures should have been realistically assessed.

As explained, the research topic was divided into categories, each containing several assessment dimensions. Thereby, the definition of these concepts was understood as a dynamic process that explicitly allowed for conceptual adjustments in the course of data collection. Tentative hypotheses were developed to predict interrelations between these concepts that formed the building blocks of the suggested theory. Corresponding with the core dimensions of the two-staged central research question, theoretical models were developed. Fig. 4.1 shows the assumed interrelationships and mechanisms of loan risk management at CRE debt funds.

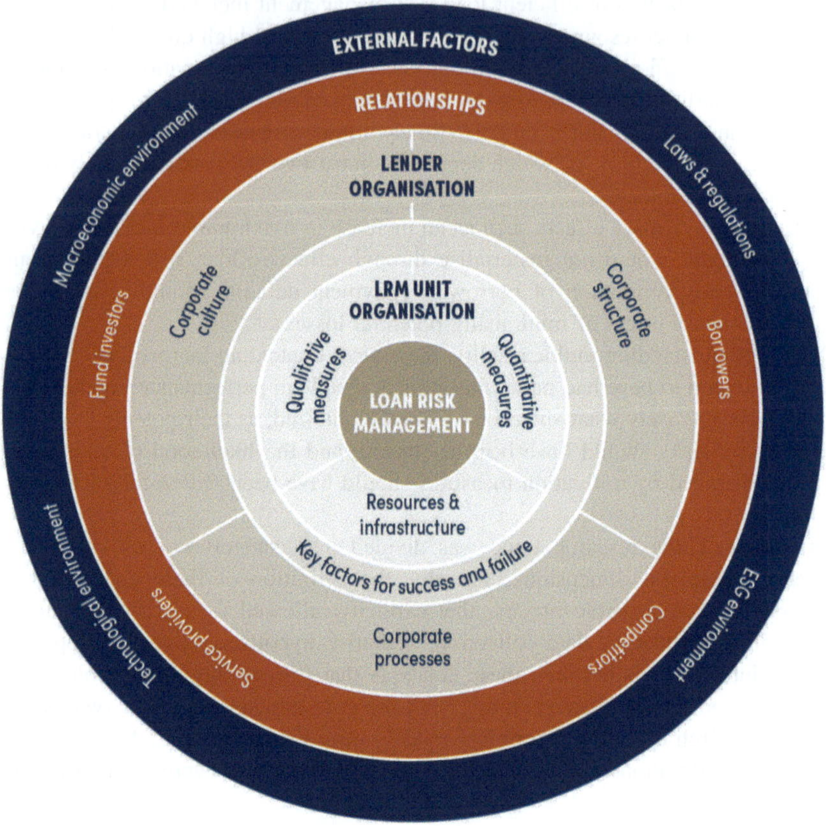

Fig. 4.1 Interrelationships and mechanisms of loan risk management. (Source: o. i.)

As discussed, the model of the theoretical impacts assumed a cause-and-effect relationship between loan risk management and loan performance. It furthermore distinguished between the proactive area of direct control and influence, and the reactive area of indirect influence. In this way, the relevant system boundary was suggested, beyond which external influencing factors were predominant. This theoretical ex-ante model, which revealed the identified core and boundary factors as areas of inquiry, is shown in Fig. 4.2.

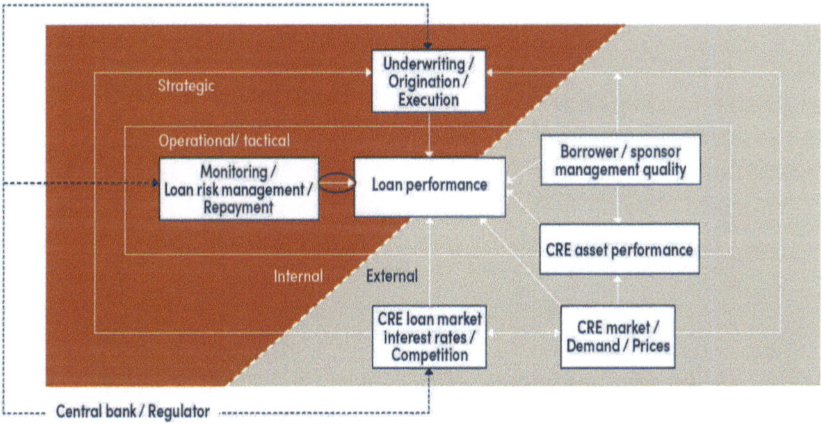

Fig. 4.2 Theoretical impact model: Loan performance determinants. (Source: o. i.)

In summary, the author's analytical questions formed the link, so to speak, between the ex-ante propositions and suggested theory, on the one hand, and the qualitative survey methods, on the other (Gläser & Laudel, 2010). The following chapter presents the research design and methodology which were considered appropriate to respond to the research questions and to test and verify the ex-ante propositions and the theoretical models.

Research Design and Methodology 5

Following the definition of key concepts and technical terms, the literature review synopsis, and the presentation of the research questions and ex-ante propositions, the research design and the methodology are introduced. This chapter presents a concise, updated version of the author's initial research proposal, which was submitted to SDA Bocconi in November 2023 (Hammel, 2023). The nature and the characteristics of qualitative research, and the reasons for choosing grounded theory for the research design, while rejecting a mixed-methods approach, are presented. As set out in detail, semi-structured expert interviews, the literature review, and systematic observations were chosen, in line with the triangulation of methods. The non-random, purposeful sample selection for semi-structured interviews is introduced, including types of sampling, criteria for selection, and the division of respondents into groups of interviewees. Types of data limitation are identified, and strategies to mitigate these and minimise bias are presented. Thereafter, data management and data analysis processes are outlined, and notes on the reliability and validity of qualitative research are shared.

5.1 Research Design

The systematic inquiry into loan management practices of CRE debt funds and their plausible impact on loan performance required a design which was sensitive to underlying processes and mechanisms. Typically, qualitative research is distinguished by three characteristics: (i) the process initially being inductive and aiming at developing theory, followed by a more deductive process of testing hypotheses; (ii) the product of inquiry being richly descriptive, rather than supported by numbers; and (iii) the design being emergent, flexible, and responsive to the changing conditions of the study process (Merriam & Tisdell, 2016).

W. Hammel, *Loan Risk Management of Commercial Real Estate Debt Funds*,
https://doi.org/10.1007/978-3-658-48912-0_5

Due to its particular efficacy in addressing questions about processes and mechanisms, grounded theory was selected for the research design. Classic grounded theory usually employs three forms of research logic: (i) inductive research as the foundational process of conceptualisation; (ii) the methodological approach of abduction for the recognition of interrelationships of major concepts to arrive at an integrated theory; and (iii) deduction for verification of the conceived theory. The author therefore followed the three-step analytical progression of induction, abduction and deduction to connect all hypotheses into a fully integrated theory (Merriam & Tisdell, 2016).

The option of applying a mixed-methods design that would have allowed for the expansion of the qualitative paradigm to quantitative analysis was ruled out. Due to the opaqueness of the business sector under review and the unfamiliarity of its being the subject of scientific research, it was assumed that an impersonal online survey would have attracted fairly low response rates. Furthermore, it was felt that such data as would have been provided would have had limited informative value due to the anticipated reluctance of respondents to provide detailed written explanations, and that qualitative survey methods—in the first instance semi-structured expert interviews—would deliver more significant results. It was assumed that satisfactory levels of familiarity would be established through personal dialogue, allowing for deeper insight into the subject matter.

5.2 Methodological Approach

In line with the triangulation of methods, three complementary data collection methods were chosen: (i) semi-structured expert interviews; (ii) a literature review; and (iii) observation. In light of the application of grounded theory, it should also be noted that the literature review and observation were primarily used in the process of theory building, and the semi-structured interviews more for theory-testing. Since the method employed for semi-structured expert interviews will be described in detail in the Sect. 5.3 below, only the qualitative methods of literature review and observation are discussed in this section.

As a systematic approach to collecting and synthesising previous research, the literature review offered a key point of reference for conceptualisation, informing the development of the building blocks of the systemic theory. In this way, the literature review provided the theoretical foundation of the research problem to be investigated, and guided the way in which this study was framed. The qualitative work of Bloom and van Reenen (2007) on measuring and explaining management practices across firms and countries was used as a blueprint for the conceptual framework of this study. For references, the Citavi© programme for academic literature management and knowledge organisation was used.

The recently concluded desk study on alternative financing of commercial property by debt funds and insurance companies should be given special mention, as it served as the cornerstone database for the survey design (Hinkel, 2024). Being limited to web-based research, and consequently publicly available data, this bachelor's thesis addressed the questions of which were the main players in this market, which key strategies were pursued, and how personnel structures, particularly for risk management, were organised. The starting point was the previously mentioned database of INREV (2023a), which only included INREV members. Further rankings, such as the list given in Real Estate Capital Europe (2023) and other online information sources, were utilised to create an overview of the most relevant debt funds in Europe. The difficulty of gaining access to sensitive data, which these companies seemed to be reluctant to publicly disclose, and the challenge of merging and comparing data scattered around different web sources were identified as Hinkel's key research limitations.

Observation was another data collection strategy designed to develop the theoretical concept and to address the research questions. The author was not just a passive observer of a group of stakeholders being surveyed, but an active member of the sector under review. Observations of the author in the context of this study were thus not limited to the data collection process, but were also based on years of professional engagement in the CRE debt universe.

In the absence of wider scientific research on the subject under review, semi-structured expert interviews formed the centrepiece of the theory-testing approach. The following chapter focuses on the types of sampling, the criteria for selection, the division of respondents into groups of interviewees, and the construction of interview guidelines tailored to suit each target group.

5.3 Survey Design, Sample Selection and Guidelines

In qualitative research, sample selection is usually non-random, purposeful, and small. Since generalisation in a statistical sense is not a goal of qualitative research, probabilistic sampling is neither necessary nor justifiable (Merriam & Tisdell, 2016). For purposeful sampling, a criterion-based selection was made. Criterion-based selection reduces research bias, as does the exploration of topics from multiple perspectives.

Data triangulation was applied through assigning interviewees to groups of respondents, which allowed for exploration from different viewpoints and perspectives. The size of the sample was determined by informational considerations, with reaching the point of saturation or redundancy as the primary criterion (Gläser & Laudel, 2010).

Two types of purposeful sampling predominated. As the first step, convenience sampling was applied, and a sample was selected based on the direct accessibility of respondents (54% of 52 cases). As the second step, snowball sampling was applied (46% of 52 cases). In essence, the strategy involved the identification of key respondents that met the established criteria, and then asking those for referrals to other potential interviewees. The key measure of success of this strategy was that respondents themselves considered participation in the interviews as beneficial, or at least sufficiently interesting, and were therefore willing to recommend participation to others. For both sampling types, the level of acquaintance between the author and his interview partners in principle held the potential for researcher's bias, as 11% of the interviewees were "well known" to the author, 31% were "fairly well known" and 37% were "somewhat known", while only 21% were "not previously known".

As well as willingness and authority to provide information, criteria for the selection of respondents included their expertise and experiences in the field under investigation, and their physical and temporal availability. Of the total number of 52 experts who were interviewed in semi-structured interviews, 11 (21%) were female and 41 (79%) male. Gender-specific selection criteria were not applied, as it was assumed that in the context of this study gender would not have a significant influence on the views expressed. Assuming a correlation between age and professional experience, the interviewees could predominantly be regarded as experienced: 58% were between 41 and 50 years old, 27% between 51 and 60, and 6% were 61 years and older. Only 10% of the respondents were 40 years old or younger. Interviewees could be divided into those based in the UK (52%), Germany (35%), and other European countries (13%), namely Denmark, Ireland, the Netherlands, and Sweden.

The division of respondents into groups of interviewees followed from the distribution of information and the need for empirical validation (see Fig. 5.1). Respondents were divided into four key groups: (i) lenders (48%); (ii) borrowers (8%); (iii) intermediaries (loan servicers, law firms) (27%); and (iv) subject matter experts (regulators, market analysts) (17%). Within those groups, further differentiation was made to collate viewpoints. Of the 25 lenders interviewed, 44% were from the strategic so-called "C level", 48% were from the (non-risk and non-compliance) operational level, and 8% performed operational risk monitoring and compliance functions. It is worth noting that about 12% of all lenders interviewed were representatives of banks. Of the four borrowers included in the survey, three (75%) were senior executives. The group of intermediaries (14 in total) included loan servicers (64%), representatives of law firms (29%) and loan brokers (7%). The diverse group of the nine subject matter experts included industry experts who were not directly involved in loan management but had sector expertise and potentially more of a "bird's eye" perspective, namely representatives of regulator/industry bodies (44%); market analysts and media professionals (23%); consultants/ advisors (22%); and auditors (11%). As it was assumed that company size would in principle correspond with resources available for loan risk management, the total of 18 CRE debt funds (with 22 respondents) included in this study could be assigned to the following groups: large debt fund managers, with more than 5 billion EUR assets under management (AUM) (18%); mid-sized debt fund managers, with 1–5 billion EUR AUM (32%); and smaller debt fund managers, with under 1 billion EUR AUM (50%).

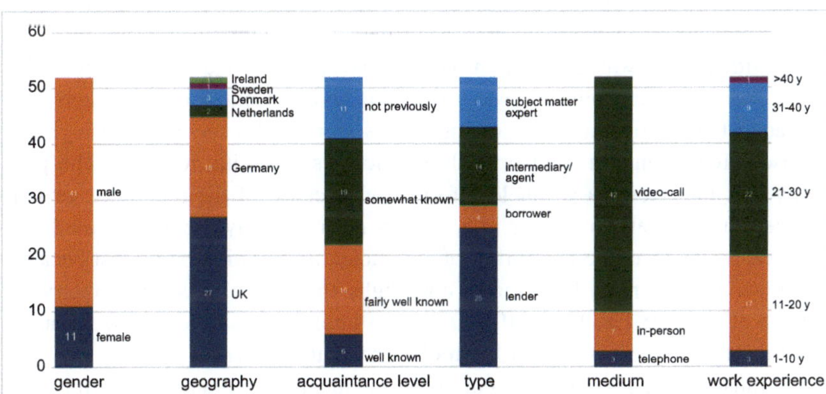

Fig. 5.1 Distribution of respondents. (Source: o. i.)

Data collection took place between February and July 2024. The interview mode was hybrid, including video communication with Microsoft Teams (81%), face-to-face conversation (13%), and telephone calls (6%). By and large, the response rate of 60% (52 out of the 87 persons contacted) was fairly high, and in only 6% (3 out of 52) of the successfully contacted cases was it necessary to follow up on the initial request.

The following types of questions were applied (Gläser & Laudel, 2010; Kromrey, 2002; Merriam & Tisdell, 2016): (i) knowledge questions; (ii) experience and behaviour questions; (iii) opinion and values questions; (iv) hypothetical questions; (v) devil's advocate questions; and (vi) ideal situation questions. As the interview guidelines were semi-structured, there was sufficient room for probes and follow-up questions.

The open-ended interview approach was complemented by a small-scale survey among respondents in semi-structured interviews. Capturing interviewees' perceptions on a five-point Likert scale (Likert, 1932) served to graphically illustrate opinions and perceptions regarding the investigated phenomena, and in no way is the survey claimed to be statistically representative.

As a rule, the analysis included not only the content of the interviews directly linked to the questions, but also additional information such as comments on how the interview came about (e.g. the degree of willingness to participate, and possible objections), and descriptions of the interview's framework conditions (e.g. duration, location, disturbing factors, interruptions).

Confidentiality was assured through non-disclosure agreements. To avoid links between statements and their originators, direct quotes have been anonymised in this publication. In the submitted academic thesis, references were encoded, and confidentiality was ensured through password-protected file servers. Prior to the interviews, the purpose was explained and consent for audio recording was requested. Altogether 96% of interviews were audio recorded through the Microsoft Teams environment or with an unobtrusive digital recorder. The possibility that interviewees withheld information because of the recording, or that they were more likely to answer in a socially desirable way, cannot be ruled out. However, on balance, the possibility of significant information being lost because interviews are not recorded usually outweighs the risk of a skewed interview situation (Gläser & Laudel, 2010). Only two interviewees objected to an audio recording. In these cases, the author took handwritten notes.

As translation errors often occur in automatically generated transcripts, the clean verbatim protocols were quality-assured by sub-contracted transcription experts following predetermined transcription rules. As the transcribed conversations included technical jargon and industry-specific language, they were provided with a glossary of terms. Clean verbatim transcription (with minor edits to remove pauses, repetitions, place-holders, etc.) was preferred, as full verbatim transcription would not have meaningfully added value.

5.4 Data Limitations and Bias Control

At the outset of the study, four types of possible data limitation were identified: (i) access to information; (ii) access to interviewees; (iii) researcher's bias; and (iv) respondents' bias. The following section discusses which data limitations of those initially identified in the author's research proposal (Hammel, 2023) proved to be relevant, and what mitigation measures were applied in these cases.

With regard to access to information, the key challenge remained that the impact of loan risk management on loan performance could not be adequately substantiated on the basis of the limited hard data that were available. As discussed, debt funds were situated in a largely opaque space, where figures and statistics were only accessible by investors, and only high-level corporate data were reported to the regulator under the AIFMD regulations. A rudimentary overview of the CRE debt universe was made available through INREV (2023a), but it only captured certain data relating to INREV members. To arrive at robust conclusions based on hard data, debt funds would have had to actually expose loan-by-loan asset information, fund level metrics such as leverage, and capital amounts invested. Since this did not happen, plausible conclusions on the causal mechanisms at play could only be drawn from experts' responses to questions relating to knowledge, experience, behaviour, and opinions. Responses to hypothetical questions about what respondents might do in a given situation, devil's advocate questions challenging respondents to consider opposing views on or explanations for a situation, and questions seeking views of ideal situations, provided relevant insights.

Through combining convenience sampling with snowball sampling, selection bias was significantly reduced. With regard to access to interviewees, sampling bias due to non-random differences in the willingness of individuals to participate was possible, albeit to a limited extent. At 60%, the overall response rate to interview requests was fairly high, and no substantial differences were found between the interviewees selected via convenience sampling and those selected via snowball sampling. Personal contacts did not automatically translate into higher willingness to participate, unless they were characterised by more intense previous working relationships. Refusal to participate among representatives of CRE debt funds that did have systematic loan risk management in place was not higher than among those that did not. In general terms, the non-participation of interview partners was more likely to be accounted for by individual characteristics. None of those who did not respond provided reasons for their non-participation. In these cases, initial and follow-up emails simply remained unanswered. Furthermore, it became apparent that even though regulatory bodies were supposed to be accessible to market participants, interview requests were confronted with comparatively high institutional hurdles.

Precisely because the author himself had been professionally active in the CRE debt fund sector and had accumulated relevant knowledge and experience over the years, both researcher's confirmation bias and analysis bias had to be consciously counteracted. The tendency to interpret data in such a way that they confirmed his own experience-based perceptions had to be controlled. Interpretations needed to be repeatedly re-evaluated to ensure that preconceived assumptions were kept in check. Consensus coding of ten percent of interview transcripts was applied as a mitigation measure, i.e., an external person cross-coded these particular transcripts in order for a comparison of findings to be made. Most importantly, however, a largely unbiased mindset was deliberately retained. Keeping the potential for multicausality in mind, the aim was not just to test whether loan risk management practices had a significant impact on loan performance, but also to identify other contributing factors that might have exerted particular influence. To arrive at plausible conclusions relating to the central causal mechanism tested, loan risk management's contributions to loan performance were ranked for comparison against other contributing and interfering factors.

The effects of participants' bias appeared to be manageable. Acquiescence bias, i.e., respondents agreeing with the researcher just to complete the interview, typically due to fatigue, was not observed. On the contrary, where there were no time constraints, respondents tended to elaborate and to overrun the scheduled interview duration of one hour by ten to twenty minutes. Social desirability bias in cases where sensitive questions on controversial topics were posed was observed among a few respondents from the middle management level who resorted to more cautious and carefully considered expressions. In the main, however, the predominant observation was that after a brief warm-up phase, most respondents spoke their minds openly, without circumlocution or embellishment.

5.5 Qualitative Data Analysis

The much-preferred way to analyse data in a qualitative study is as far as possible to do so while the data is being collected. Without ongoing analysis, data can be unfocussed and overwhelming, given the volume of material to be processed (Merriam & Tisdell, 2016). Even though the bulk of the data were only analysed after the collection had been completed, the first few interviews served as a trial run, leading to amendments to the interview guidelines.

Thematic analysis was used to identify patterns of meaning, thereby revealing implicit concepts and themes within the data. Thematic analysis was chosen because it accommodates both inductive and deductive approaches, thereby allowing for flexibility in the research framework. In the data management and analysis process, the author employed the predefined set of core categories and assessment dimensions that were introduced in Sect. 4.2. However, allowance was made for flexibility, and categories and assessment dimensions were reviewed throughout the process of data collection to enable the introduction of new and important material that could have significant implications. This meant that the author progressed from inductive and abductive approaches, where data items were assigned to tentative categories and dimensions, to a stronger deductive approach, where more evidence was sought in support of a final set of categories and dimensions (Gläser & Laudel, 2010; Merriam & Tisdell, 2016).

To manage qualitative data from interview transcripts, textual data were analysed using descriptive codes which corresponded with the predefined categories and assessment dimensions. For the purpose of thematic analysis, the computer-assisted qualitative data analysis software ATLAS.ti was used. To allow for the identification of patterns in meaning across the data set, interview transcripts were imported in the ATLAS.ti repository. Coding in ATLAS.ti provided for the marking of more than 2,700 text segments with the abovementioned descriptive codes. For data analysis, relevant text passages from all interview transcripts were thus accessed and grouped. Coding was performed for the presence of themes or concepts, on the one hand, and on the other, for number of appearances in text (Friese, 2019; Woods et al., 2016). To identify the key lines of reasoning and argumentation, connections were made between occurrences and the significance of what had been shared (Gläser & Laudel, 2010).

Extracting the required information allowed for the consolidation, reduction and interpretation of text-based data. First and foremost, the data analysis aimed to answer the central research question, i.e., to verify the posited causal mechanism between practices of loan risk management and loan performance. In this way, causality was examined at three different levels of abstraction (Gläser & Laudel, 2010): (i) the views and experiences of the interviewees on interrelationships and mechanisms; (ii) the author's reconstruction of the described contexts and mechanisms, bearing in mind influencing factors; and (iii) the comparative analysis of commonalities and differences, and the occurrence of factors, causes and conditions. In order to answer the research questions, the empirical findings had thus to be confronted with the ex-ante propositions, which were tested.

Finally, the author would like to add some notes on the reliability and validity of qualitative research, based on the most relevant thoughts of Merriam and

Tisdell (2016). As qualitative research is based on assumptions about reality, the standards of rigor necessarily differ from those applied in quantitative research. One of the assumptions underlying qualitative research is that reality is not a single, fixed and objective phenomenon waiting to be discovered, but is holistic, multidimensional, and everchanging. As human beings are the primary instrument of data collection and analysis in qualitative research, interpretations of reality are accessed directly through interviews and observations. That is why it is important to understand the perspectives of those involved, to uncover the complexity of human behaviour, and to present a holistic interpretation. The best-known strategies to shore up validity and increase credibility are triangulations of both methods and data. Adequate time spent collecting data that might support the tested causal mechanism was coupled with purposeful searching for variations in the understanding of the phenomena. The analytical findings derived from data retrieved during the data collection process are presented in the following chapter.

Research Findings 6

In this core chapter of the study, the research findings are presented. This chapter is oriented towards the dimensions of the two-staged central research question: What were the loan risk management practices of CRE debt funds, and what effects did these practices plausibly have on loan performance? Keeping the possibility of multicausality in mind, the mechanism presented in this research question assumed a cause-and-effect relationship. As this investigation should do justice to the complexity of the processes involved, the first two subchapters were further structured into sections that focussed on key criteria and their underlying assessment dimensions. The division of the research topic into various categories and dimensions assisted the designing of the target group-specific questionnaire for semi-structured expert interviews, as respondents' varying abilities to provide information from different perspectives and viewpoints were considered. With the application of data triangulation, this systematic approach ensured an equal confrontation of the ex-ante propositions with the empirical findings. Views on and experiences with interrelationships and mechanisms were captured, and contexts and mechanisms were reconstructed, taking account of influencing factors.

The third subchapter presents the findings of a small-scale survey which aimed to complement the open-ended qualitative research by capturing respondents' views on a five-point Likert scale. While it is in no way claimed that the findings of this small-scale survey are statistically representative, respondents' agreement or disagreement with selected statements illustrate opinions and perceptions on the investigated phenomena. With the proviso that extremely narrow limits to robust and reliable analysis were imposed by the scarcity of referenceable academic research and the lack of statistically significant quantitative data, a reflective account of the posited macroeconomic impacts of debt funds' loan performance is presented in the fourth subchapter.

W. Hammel, *Loan Risk Management of Commercial Real Estate Debt Funds*,
https://doi.org/10.1007/978-3-658-48912-0_6

6.1 Loan Risk Management Practices of CRE Debt Funds

This subchapter on loan risk management practices responds to the first dimension of the two-staged central research question: What were the loan risk management practices of CRE debt funds? Examining the organisational level of debt funds, the first section of this subchapter is divided along sections addressing the following assessment dimensions: (i) corporate structures; (ii) corporate processes; (iii) corporate cultures; and (iv) interorganisational relationships. The second section of this subchapter is devoted to the operational implementation in the responsible units at debt funds, along the following assessment dimensions: (i) resources and infrastructure; (ii) quantitative measures; and (iii) qualitative measures. The subchapter is rounded off with brief concluding remarks.

6.1.1 Lender-level Loan Risk Management

This section is dedicated to lender-level loan risk management. First, findings are presented on the extent to which corporate structures of debt funds created more or less favourable conditions for effective loan risk management, and on how loan risk management units were anchored in these corporate structures. Then the question of how loan risk management was integrated in the corporate processes of debt funds is addressed, before findings are presented on the question of whether corporate cultures determined attitudes and behaviours towards risk management, and if so, in what way. Finally, the key characteristics of interorganisational relationships between lenders, borrowers, service providers and investors, and the extent to which these determined the effectiveness of loan risk management, are addressed.

6.1.1.1 Corporate Structures

This section aims to answer two second-tier research questions: firstly, the extent to which corporate structures of debt funds created more or less favourable conditions for effective loan management; and secondly, the ways in which loan risk management units were anchored in these corporate structures. The analysis took account of the fact that CRE debt funds were by no means a homogenous group but varied considerably. It is precisely this diversity that raised questions about relational connections between funds' sizes and structures, on the one hand, and the endowment of their loan risk units, on the other.

In the narrower sense, the term "debt fund" refers to a limited partnership fund vehicle which holds certain individual loans as its investments, and into which investors put their capital as limited partners. These limited partnerships are managed by a general partner, who is the investment manager of the fund, often but not always regulated under applicable law. In the EU context, the investment manager is regulated under the AIFMD (European Parliament Directive 2011/61-AIFMD I, 2011; European Parliament Regulation 231/2013—AIFMD/CDR, 2012; European Parliament, Directive 2024/927—AIFMD II, 2024) and is referred to as the AIFM. In certain cases, the sponsor of the fund does not itself hold an AIFM license. Instead an external AIFM (often referred to as "service AIFM" or "host AIFM") fronts the fund and outsources certain responsibilities to the debt fund sponsor, such as sourcing, underwriting, transaction management and monitoring (alfi, 2014). In such cases, the sponsor (and often name-giver) of the debt fund acts as a service provider to the AIFM. Outsourcing of certain tasks provided paths for smaller funds to operate under the umbrella of an existing AIFM and to perform so-called key value-creating roles. This practise was, however, criticised by the Financial Conduct Authority (FCA, 2024) for being prone to a lack of clarity in the division of responsibilities, and to having insufficient oversight mechanisms in place.

In the broader sense, the term "debt fund" is used in connection with the sponsor as the organisational backbone and the so-called face to the customer. In this study, the term was used in this broader sense, as the thesis was focussed on the organisational structures and operations of lenders, rather than on technical aspects of individual investment vehicles. It must be borne in mind, however, that single sponsors often managed multiple investment vehicles which were set up with differing investment foci for specific investment types and with certain investor groups in mind.

In the broader understanding of the lender organisation, debt funds can be categorised in the following investment management types: (i) stand-alone; (ii) investment manager-related; (iii) investment bank-related; (iv) insurance-related; and (v) private equity-related. The investment focus of these debt funds is either the origination of debt or the purchasing of debt in the market. Debt funds can be further distinguished on the basis of their business areas, such as loan types, geographic focus, asset classes, and asset categories. Loan types include (i) senior loans; (ii) whole loans; (iii) mezzanine/junior loans; (iv) preferred equity loans; and (v) bridge loans. European debt funds usually differ with respect to the following geographical foci: (i) single country; (ii) pan-European; (iii) EU core countries plus UK; (iv) southern Europe; and (v) eastern Europe. The following asset classes are typically distinguished: (i) office; (ii) retail; (iii) multi-family housing; (iv) logistics; (v) hotel; (vi) student housing; and (vii) care home. Asset categories include (i) investment properties; (ii) development properties; (iii) transformational properties; (iv) operating properties; and (v) land acquisitions. Company sizes are usually defined by loan ticket sizes in EUR or GBP (Great Britain Pounds): (i) <1 million; (ii) 1–5 million; (iii) 5–25 million; (iv) 25–100 million; and (v) >100 million. Apart from the allocation to business areas and company sizes, the investment management types of debt funds can be grouped according to their typological structures, forms of capital raising, and investment decisions. Fig. 6.1 shows this structural categorisation of debt funds by investment management type and provides an assessment of corresponding advantages and disadvantages.

	Description/ structure	Capital raising	Investment decisions	Advantages/ disadvantages
Stand-alone	Manager is owned by partners / founders	Disproportionate effort to raise funds	Hands-on approach, responsibility of leadership team, fast and flexible	High degree of specialisation and autonomy, team size, insufficient economies of scale
Investment manager-related	Part of a larger investment manager organisation	Economies of scale, access to existing investors for multiple products	Institutional with multiple committees	Economies of scale for certain administration and risk functions
Investment bank-related	Connected to a (often US) investment bank	Utilisation of bank platform, access to investment bank clients and „bank DNA" perception	Institutional with multiple committees	Entrepreneurial with "bank style" governance
Insurance-related	Connected to an insurance company	Access to insurance funds	Institutional with multiple committees	Access to capital, potentially longer-term view, robust governance
Private equity-related	Often part of an established private equity investment manager	Access to existing private equity clients, "CRE experts" perception	Private equity-approach, with intensive due diligence, often similar process as for equity decisions	Hands-on private equity-approach, CRE expertise, conflict of interest

Fig. 6.1 Categorisation of debt funds by manager type. (Source: o. i.)

In the alternative lending market, there were indications of market consolidation in progress, with a tendency for institutional and established debt funds to drive out or take over smaller, less established ones. During market upswings, so-called sunshine funds had emerged. Some of these small and medium-sized debt funds had not succeeded in establishing themselves by passing certain thresholds of total loan volume, or AUM, by periods of economic downswing and the consequent setting in of market adjustment processes. Market shocks such as the then-recent interest rate hikes influenced the behaviour of institutional investors, which increasingly withdrew from CRE debt exposures.

> *Debt funds will continue to increase the market share of the CRE finance market. I can see the big debt funds getting stronger, while some smaller funds may struggle to raise capital and deploy it effectively. There is a flight to quality in terms of investors turning to more established funds, so they seem to get bigger and stronger.*
>
> *Senior manager, loan servicer, UK*

The types of investment management determined the manner in which debt funds were structured, how they operated, and how they were perceived in the market. As volume seemed to drive change in the alternative funding market, company size was a key determinant of corporate structure. The bureaucratic procedures of larger, institutional debt funds became increasingly similar to those of traditional financial institutions. As they tended to lose appetite for mezzanine and junior loans, their preferred loan types also gradually came to resemble those of banks. Small and medium-sized debt funds, in particular, were valued for their time-efficient decision-making processes. Their ability to quickly adopt positions on transactions was seen as a competitive advantage. However, their higher exposure to concentration risks was problematical.

Of particular interest for this study was the functional separation of loan origination from loan risk management, which was a requirement for CRE debt funds under the AIFMD regulation. While most debt funds in the EU and the UK were AIFM-regulated, they did have the option of being classed as so-called regulated lenders, in which case they would fall under the supervisory authority of national banking regulators, i.e. BaFin in Germany or the CSSF (Commission de Surveillance du Secteur Financier) in Luxembourg (KPMG, 2022). Subject to certain exceptions, debt funds that did not require EU-based investors and had been set up either onshore in the UK, near-offshore (e.g. Guernsey) or far-offshore (e.g. Cayman Islands) could lend without any regulatory oversight in the EU or the UK.

Larger debt funds had typically built up appropriate structures for loan risk management, although this did not preclude the contracting of third-party loan servicers or external restructuring experts. The larger loan ticket sizes of institutional debt funds also did not preclude a certain imbalance in staffing between front offices and back offices.

At the end, the focus is more on investing the money than on getting the money back [...], no matter whether [debt funds] are large or small. But in fact, the large funds can fall back on the structures they have in case of doubt [...] And if you are a small fund that is still in the development stage, you have just waited a little longer before investing in your structures.

Senior manager, borrower, Netherlands

While building functional loan asset and risk management units generally seemed to be a matter of corporate scale, real estate market upswings were not particularly conducive to prioritising increases in back-office staffing levels.

They have scaled back their workout departments in recent years and are now struggling to some extent. They now have to see how they build up their capacities. We have heard that some are temporarily moving their people from origination to workout, to deal with immediate problems. And of course that is not necessarily a long-term solution either [...] But I think that is a typical development. In good years you cut back, and when things get tough you need people again.

Senior manager, loan servicer, Germany

During the CRE downturn, smaller debt funds in particular often found themselves in the precarious situation of having neither sufficient in-house resources to mitigate loan defaults nor the budget to contract workout and restructuring experts. Frequently, smaller debt funds did not have separate loan management functions, so effectively the same staff who were closing deals were responsible for loan asset management. However, the functional separation between origination, underwriting and loan management was widely regarded as best practice in order to avoid conflicts of interest and operational blindness.

My personal view is that originators should not be involved after the loan is agreed [...] If somebody originated the loan [...] they should step away from the transaction. There should be an independent closing of that loan by an independent [underwriting] team [...] And then, after the loan is closed, the loan management should be done by another completely separated team [...] That was one of the [lessons] that came out of the GFC [...] As when the loan starts to fall into non-performing, the originator might have some bias towards it, and would not necessarily take the action that needs to be taken.

Senior manager, loan servicer, UK

The so-called cradle-to-grave process did not uniformly attract such a negative response, however, and by some it was seen as effective relationship management with borrowers that allowed for keeping an eye on new business opportunities.

As a critical company size was required for successfully balancing the raising of capital through new deals against the management of existing loans, leanly staffed debt funds often commissioned external loan servicers, in some cases provided that these costs were partly borne by borrowers.

> *It may be that such special vehicles are unable to properly manage the arbitrage between [economic] pressure and internal administration. Of course, you only see this when the tide goes out. Then you see who went swimming without their trunks. The workout capacity and the crisis management capacity tend to be lower in smaller [debt funds] than in larger ones. Dragging along a workout department as fixed costs is neither lean nor efficient. And if you want to outsource it, you need cash flow.*
>
> *Senior manager, law firm, Germany*

Loan administration provided by external loan servicers should thus be understood as tasks preceding the governance-function of in-house loan risk management. While the activity of loan servicing might be outsourced, this did not apply to the overall responsibility for loan management.

Some small and medium-sized debt funds were purchased by larger platforms as part of strategic sales or takeovers. Acquirers with pre-existing infrastructure typically offered additional resources for risk management, legal counselling, compliance, and internal auditing.

In order to better understand the anchoring of risk management in the corporate structures of debt funds and the consequent assignment of roles and responsibilities, the use of terminology was examined. The discussion of conceptual and functional distinctions between asset management and risk management was also of particular interest. The study examined the extent to which the widespread avoidance of the term "risk" on company websites was reflected in the reluctance to use this term for operational units. The recently concluded desk study on alternative financing of commercial property pointed out that only 16% of 50 surveyed debt funds and insurance companies portrayed their companies' risk management functions on their websites by introducing the responsible units and staff members (Hinkel, 2024). The reason for this might be that these debt funds did not want to be subconsciously associated with high-risk loans or loans already marked by some kind of distressed status.

In the absence of industry-wide nomenclature, the terms most widely used were "loan management", followed by "loan asset management" and "portfolio management", and merely "asset management". Frequently, overarching designations included various sub-functions, such as loan management incorporating asset management, or asset management including loan surveillance, loan administration and finances. Only in exceptional cases was the term "risk" included in overarching department names, and instead it was mentioned as an incorporated field of responsibility. The terms "loan administration" and "loan surveillance" were frequently associated with external loan servicing. The distinction between "portfolio management", relating to entire loan portfolios, and "loan management", referring to the individual loan level, was treated inconsistently. Interestingly, risk monitoring as an overview function was sometimes associated with portfolio management rather than with loan management.

As for the conceptual and functional distinction between "asset management" and "risk management", there were different schools of thought. The inclination to separate the two areas of work seems to be related not only to capital and resources, but also to respective risk profiles. Distinctions were drawn between the administrative tasks of loan management, including the supervision of processes as the responsibility of borrowers and loan servicers, and more analytical risk management tasks, such as stress testing, scenario and watchlist analysis, and workout of defaulted positions. Some debt funds saw the function of risk management as not necessarily being assigned only to back offices. Rather, the function was understood as falling under the cross-departmental tasks of credit risk officers who monitor loans from origination and underwriting through to management. This allowed for the flagging of issues and further investigation, as required.

For the purposes of this study, the term "loan risk management" was used to standardise the varied professional nomenclature used by debt funds. The usage of the term should also be understood as a plea for the introduction of standardised definitions for the roles and responsibilities of the loan risk management function. Furthermore, this study refers to "loan risk management units", even though it emerged that many debt funds did not have such designated operational units in place, and that this function was instead partly or fully outsourced to loan servicers, or taken on by individual staff members, or both.

Following this discussion of the extent to which corporate structures set conditions for loan risk management, attention now turns to processes as further components of debt fund governance systems.

6.1.1.2 Corporate Processes

This section addresses the sub-question of how loan risk management was integrated in the corporate processes of debt funds. The analysis took account of the fact that the distinction between intra- and inter-organisational processes was not entirely clearcut, as borrowers, loan servicers and investors were regularly involved.

The section distinguishes between four different types of corporate process which were delineated for the purposes of the study. As shown in Table 6.1, the lines of distinction ran between integration and segregation of front and back offices, on the one hand, and the assignment or non-assignment of external loan servicers, on the other. As shown in the previous section, company size proved to be a key determinant for the structures of debt funds, and in turn also conditioned processes.

Table 6.1 Process types of debt funds.

	Integrated	Segregated
With loan servicer	Process type A	Process type C
Without loan servicer	Process type B	Process type D

Source: o. i.

Process type A operated in lean corporate structures with no clear personnel and functional separation between front and back offices, where external servicers had been assigned for loan risk monitoring. Process type B represented the same integrated process type without a clear functional separation, but with the task of credit risk management not being outsourced to external loan service providers. Process type C implied a clear functional and personnel separation between origination, underwriting and management, with a third-party servicer being commissioned. Finally, process type D exhibited the same kind of functional and personnel separation, with risk monitoring being carried out solely in-house. There were two distinct variants for the two latter process types: either with the assignment of the credit risk function only to asset management, or with the assignment of an independent cross-departmental function. Of particular interest was whether risk managers had a veto right, meaning the right to object within a formally defined framework and thus to postpone or block decisions. Regarding the assignment of processes to types, it should also be mentioned that the distinction between integrated and segregated approaches was not always clearcut, as in some cases the originator remained principally or secondarily responsible for the loan, even though an asset management unit had been established.

Regardless of the process type, debt funds typically went through five successive loan phases: (i) origination; (ii) underwriting; (iii) execution; (iv) asset and risk management; and (v) redemption as ordinary course or workout and restructuring. These phases are presented in Fig. 6.2, with consideration of the specifications of process types.

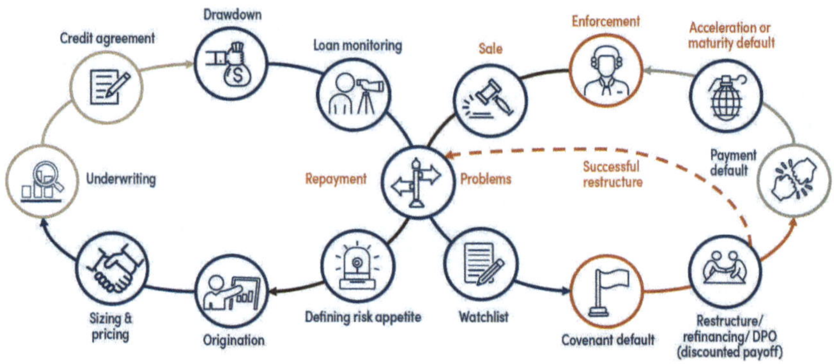

Fig. 6.2 Loan stage phases. (Source: o. i.)

During the origination phase, business relationships between lenders and borrowers were initiated. Whether approaches were initially made primarily by lenders or borrowers was widely influenced by the respective competitive conditions in the CRE market. While during the so-called borrower-market phase, lender initiative was usually more pronounced, the current lender-market saw borrowers more frequently knocking on doors.

> *We are currently seeing that we are getting an enormous number of inquiries [...] I think the position of borrowers looking for financing is rather weak at the moment compared to the position of lenders. I think that the debt funds that are still actively offering real estate loans in Germany can go cherry picking.*
>
> *Senior manager, loan servicer, Germany*

Non-discretionary investments imply that investors should grant their authorisation to capital expenditure. In discretionary accounts, lenders (i.e. managers of the debt fund) are permitted to exercise their own discretion and make investments without prior permission. To ensure that financial allocations are made to companies that are regarded as trustworthy and, thereby, to limit potential losses, not only should properties be valued, but the creditworthiness of borrowers should also be assessed. Ideally, risk managers should be involved in background checks at early stages of investment review processes, before time and resources are spent on these opportunities.

The extent to which this took place depended on available resources and on whether lenders' processes tended to be more transaction-driven and property-related, or more relationship-driven in the sense of being primarily based on trustworthy customer relationships.

In the transitional period leading to the underwriting phase, investment opportunities were presented to so-called green light committees. These committees usually consisted of senior management teams of the particular debt funds. In some cases, independent internal or external credit risk officers could exercise veto rights and, if needed, file objections while reporting directly to investors. Once required budgets were approved, systematic external due diligence assessments were carried out from legal and tax perspectives, as well as from technical, economic and environmental perspectives. In line with the dual control principle, these assessments should ideally be administered by specified underwriting teams, but this was not always the case. During the underwriting phase, it would be beneficial for loan risk managers to share lessons learnt from administered loan portfolios, but this was not done across the board. The early involvement of risk management could also serve to mitigate the often-present so-called deal bias, from which even senior management teams were not entirely exempt. Depending on whether investments were discretionary or non-discretionary, senior management ultimately made decisions irrespective of prior investor approval.

Before transactions can be completed, certain conditions as requirements of agreements of purchase and sale should be met. Credit analysis processes should not just deal with the creditworthiness of borrowers, but should also consider potential losses from non-performance and potential bad debt. Lenders should weigh these risks against anticipated benefits such as RAROC (risk-adjusted return on capital).

Relating to the methods of fulfilment, two types of condition emerged: (i) conditions precedent that had to be fulfilled by a specific deadline for the deal to close, i.e. payment of the funds; and (ii) subsequent conditions that would be determined by a future event that, if it occurred, would give rise to contractual consequences, i.e. price adjustments or termination. Covenants are contractual credit conditions set by lenders which borrowers must fulfil on a regular basis during loan cycles. It was stated that they served to protect creditors and to reduce their financial and credit risks. Lenders' requirements for borrower reporting were defined, usually on a quarterly basis for investment properties, and on a monthly basis for development properties. There were different schools of thought on outsourcing key governance functions of loan administration and servicing to intermediary loan servicing agencies. To some extent decisions were based on debt funds' loan ticket sizes and staffing levels. In cases of investment loans, loan amounts were typically fully released at the beginning of terms, whereas development loans were usually paid out gradually over the loan terms, depending on the meeting of certain milestones.

Whether interaction with borrowers was handed over entirely to loan asset management units or remained in the purview of front offices (who would continue to be primarily or only partially involved) depended on the staffing levels of the company and its philosophy, values and priorities.

> *For me, it is very important that originators have a role in the ongoing management of loans [...] Generally, they will be talking to the client about new business anyway [...] In difficult situations, having the originator as the 'good cop' and the loan asset manager as the 'bad cop' can be valuable. The asset manager delivers difficult messages while the originator remains [in] a positive relationship with the client. The best originators ask what you want them to do and are humble enough to follow guidance. Ego can lead to poor decisions if the originator acts independently.*
>
> *Loan manager, lender, UK*

Loan-level risk management should include numerous tasks, including the testing of negotiated numerical and information covenants and the monitoring of a wider set of parameters, thereby functioning as an early warning mechanism. The information provided by borrowers or loan servicers in fairly standard reporting cycles was administratively processed and analysed. In internal quarterly reports, findings were presented to investment committees of senior management. In exceptional cases, investment committees were externalised to protect businesses from the previously mentioned deal bias of senior management. An innovative approach was to conduct feedback catchup sessions with borrowers following the investment committee meetings. This allowed for the mutual exchange of information and the fostering of sound relationships. Reporting to investors by senior management usually took place on a quarterly basis, typically without the direct involvement of loan risk management units. In addition to the quarterly reporting cycles, some debt funds had also introduced annual portfolio review processes. In view of the complexity of decision-making processes, in order to maximise efficiency, day-to-day operational and strategic credit decisions should ideally be systematically assigned to different levels of the corporate hierarchy. However, while decision-making processes should have been categorised and standardised through the use of approval matrices, in practice this varied, and not all cases were accorded equal and satisfactory consideration.

Either debt was paid in the ordinary course of business as per contractual obligations or loan payment default occurred, i.e. borrowers failed to make the required interest or principal redemption payments on debts. The review of SPLs, or even more so, NPLs, naturally required more frequent reviews by investment committees. Real estate loan restructuring involved modifying the terms of existing loan agreements to accommodate changing financial circumstances or to address default risks. Consensual restructuring arrangements varied widely depending on the specific needs of borrowers and lenders. Common strategies included (i) term extension; (ii) interest rate adjustment; (iii) principal reduction; (iv) payment deferrals; and (v) equity injection. While the primary route for any restructuring should be consensual, failure to reach agreement in this regard resulted in the enforcement of non-consensual restructuring plans, including mortgage or share pledge enforcement and insolvency.

Following this presentation of the types of corporate process along the staged loan phases, attention now turns to corporate cultures as determining factors for attitudes, behaviours and decision-making.

6.1.1.3 Corporate Cultures

In this section, findings are presented on the second-tier research question regarding whether corporate cultures determined attitudes and behaviours towards risk management, and if so, in what ways. Cultural patterns resulted from the interplay of values, norms, mindsets and paradigms that have been frequently observed in the CRE debt fund lending space. It was accordingly recognised that the degree of prevalence and the depth of anchoring of these cultural patterns naturally varied. The conditions created by the corporate environment of alternative lending were naturally taken into account. Competition for origination of new loans was high, and margins were comparatively low. The lean organisational structure of many funds set limits on the outlays for units that are supposedly "non-revenue", but which do in fact indirectly generate revenue. This section also deals with the extent to which the required skill sets for loan risk management were recognised in both the recruitment and the renumeration of personnel. Finally, attitudes and beliefs were also widely observed among current and potential employees, which made recruitment to the units responsible for loan risk management more challenging. These considerations are based solely on anecdotal observations of the experts surveyed.

After the GFC, the alternative lending space emerged and took on asset classes, capital structures and geographic regions from which more strictly regulated traditional banks had withdrawn. With their stronger entrepreneurial spirit and more pronounced risk appetite, debt funds quickly expanded into the market to deploy capital and create attractive returns for investors. These debt funds were often founded by influential and well-connected personalities that had gained prior experience in the banking sector. The market welcomed and stimulated risk-taking in the alternative lending space, while regulators simultaneously prevented banks from taking up such positions in order to reduce systemic risks. Before the heated markets were forced to cool down due the significant impacts of more recent global crises, the focus had primarily been on origination, in the sense of bringing in deals, making profits and maintaining the pipeline through constant capital raising.

> *Nowadays you only do new business if you can still breathe on the risk side. Today, it is all about: How to deal with these cases? How do you get the money back?*
>
> *Industry expert, Germany*

Larger funds were more able to fall back on established corporate structures in the event of loan defaults and often had sufficient capital to soften shocks. While being able to manage their loan positions during economic upcycles, smaller funds often seemed to reach the boundaries of their organisational resilience due to their limited resources and lean corporate structures, with thin personnel covers.

> *Not only because you were suddenly left with an underlying asset that is worth less, but it is more [than that], liquidity [issues] again, where if the market puts the brakes on your exit quite often [it requires] refinance, and that falls away quite quickly [...] You have got a combination of asset value dropping, market hesitancy and lack of liquidity to replace your debt. You know, it can spiral quite quickly, quite unpleasantly.*
>
> *Partner in a law firm, UK*

Some funds discerned the signs of the times early, and to minimise losses, enforced decisions even in the face of scepticism and opposition. Others tended rather to bury their heads in the sand, thereby avoiding making unpleasant disclosures to investors that might reflect badly on the debt funds' performance. Certain disaster myopia, defined as the cognitive dissonance of ignoring risks that appear to be less likely than they actually are (Herring & Wachter, 1998), seemed to have taken hold.

> *I find it interesting how few reacted and tried to reduce their exposure, to syndicate or sell, and simply sat it out, just to be confronted with an irreparable pile of shards [...] Theoretically, one could have seen during the [Covid] pandemic that home office worked quite well. And then one could have said: 'Well, maybe we will not do so much office [investments] after all'.*
>
> *Senior manager, loan servicer, Germany*

A factor which should not be underestimated is the role of certain confirmation bias (Kahneman, 2015), a tendency to confirm that an investment was indeed a good one, even in spite of evidence to the contrary which casts doubt on the soundness of the judgement behind the decision.

> *I think it is probably a negative thing overall because nobody wants to be proven wrong. I saw a deal default recently. Badly. And it was obvious that it was going to default for absolutely ages. But the person that had originated the deal, that was in charge of the asset management team as well, was effectively in denial. And that was where the issue lay [...] You look at it and you thought that it was never going to happen. So, whether this is wishful thinking or wearing rose-tinted glasses, I do not know, but there is definitely some bias in there because nobody wants to say: 'Oh look, I bought into that deal, and it was absolutely awful'.*
>
> *Senior manager, loan servicer, UK*

It stood to reason that the costs incurred for maintaining a loan risk management unit should have been in reasonable proportion to the number of loans managed, so that administrative costs could be shared. The same applied to outsourcing to service providers, which usually saved on personnel costs. At so-called tipping points of corporate growth, the awareness of the need for these operational structures seemed to increase. For smaller companies in the growth phase, the challenge would be not to miss the moment when event-driven risk management should be transformed into a more structured undertaking. There seemed to be a widespread understanding of front offices being revenue centres and value drivers, while back offices were frequently regarded as cost setters with tight budgets.

> *It is ironic because the most important thing is getting the money back. However, these businesses focus on getting the money out, hoping that everything will work out with minimal investment.*

Industry expert, UK

Even if valid strictly from a cost-calculation point of view, this seems to involve a logical error. Instead of being about maximising profit, loan risk management should be recognised as protecting the downside through proactive measures before things go awry. Proactive measures could also make economic sense in terms of saving on the sometimes exorbitant costs of legal advisors and restructuring specialists in the event of loan defaults. Suggestions were made as to how loan risk management units could better demonstrate performance-related returns. For high yield loans, in particular, additional consent fees for the account of the borrower (waiver fees and extension fees) could be charged for workout and restructuring tasks. The revenue potential of loan risk management should also take into account the fact that investors frequently rewarded good performance of debt funds with special remuneration, so-called "promotes".

> *If you could integrate special servicing skills into primary servicing to spot issues early, you could reduce losses and charge more for a forward-looking primary servicing role [...] The problem is if people make profit operating the way they do, why would anyone change? They will not until disruption forces them to.*
>
> *Industry expert, UK*

Differing cultural mindsets between the front office and the back office were observed. In order to close deals, originators would naturally have to be more optimistically inclined, while more cautious loan risk managers were at times perceived as naysayers.

> *As long as things go well, everyone is happy. If things are no longer going well, then the market side has drunk the bubbly, and the others now have to deal with it.*
>
> *Senior manager, loan servicer, Germany*

Although the required profiles for loan risk managers were actually extensive, entry-level qualifications seemed to be widely perceived as being somewhat lower than in the more competitive field of origination. Critical voices pointed out that being a loan risk manager was probably less of a dream job to which university graduates aspired. Rewards for originators typically outweighed those for loan risk managers, while renumeration was regarded as a key factor for attracting and retaining talent. Not only cross-sectoral technical skills but also soft skills required for the job were described as being often underappreciated in the industry.

So, I think the grass definitely looks greener on the origination side of the fence, when you are wearing an asset manager's hat.

Senior manager, loan servicer, UK

Conversely, inadequate appreciation was held to be responsible for the fact that qualified personnel tend to regard loan management as kind of a learning ground or stepping stone, from which to move on.

It definitely requires a specific skill set and mentality. If you can keep a loan manager in a set for more than three years, that is generally considered a very good achievement.

Senior manager, loan servicer, UK

The perceptions of back offices ranged from monotonous routine jobs with no decision-making power, to jobs with little room for creativity and less visibility in the company and the wider CRE market.

The perception of loan asset management is that it is a career path for those in the latter stages of their careers, after ten or twenty years in origination, who want to work fewer hours.

Loan manager, lender, UK

In times of economic upturn, fewer workout personnel were employed, and often when responsible persons retired, positions were not backfilled. For non-performing exposures, external restructuring experts were often hired to fill the gaps and pull the cart out of the mud, as the saying goes. As CRE debt funds were likely to expand their risk management structures in response to the increase in problematic exposures, it can be assumed that both the demand for and appreciation of professionals with experience in special servicing, workout and restructuring would grow.

We are, as everybody else is, seeing more distress or more watchlist certainty and higher LTV ratios, more valuation decrease as a result of the macro climate. I think it just shines a light on asset management. Which in good times probably just gets hidden and I think that is good and bad. It is good because it raises the profile of people in asset management, and it focuses the whole business on an area of operations that is important. But it is a shame almost, that it takes a bad point in the market for the attention to be there [...] It probably is cyclical because when the market comes back originators will bump up again, won't they? And asset management will be forgotten, and it will be a back-office function again.

Loan manager, lender, UK

The current shift in recognition could also contribute to changing the perception of loan risk management, which could arguably be much less monotonous than suggested by its reputation.

The discussion of corporate cultures is now followed by an overview of the interorganisational relationships of CRE debt funds.

6.1.1.4 Lender-Level: Interorganisational Relationships

In the following, the focus is shifted from the intra-organisational to the interorganisational level. This section addresses the key characteristics of relationships of CRE debt funds with borrowers and service providers, in particular, but also with their investors, and the extent to which these relationships determined the effectiveness of loan risk management. Since various structural, procedural and operational interrelationships are explained in other sections, the following is primarily concerned with presenting relevant external stakeholders and their responsibilities and interests (see Fig. 6.3).

The term "borrower" can be defined in two ways: either in the broader sense, which includes the sponsor as an organisational entity, or in the narrower sense, which refers only to the borrowing vehicle, often referred to as a special purpose vehicle (SPV). The terminology in this study follows the broader understanding. In terms of typology, a distinction can be drawn between private borrowers, which constituted the vast majority, and public borrowers, which were less common. Among private borrowers, a distinction is made between larger institutional investors with more professional organisational structures, e.g. investment funds, and smaller non-institutional investors that usually operated in a less bureaucratic manner, e.g. family offices. Some exchange-listed borrowers were subject to stricter regulations. Ideally, both lenders and borrowers should share an interest in maintaining trust-based relations characterised by mutual respect, readiness to compromise, and transparent and proactive communication.

> *Getting your money back is pretty key. Getting your money back in a way that means you have not killed your prospects in the market generally [...] You are in a dynamic marketplace. You need to think four or five years ahead. If you are in a downturn at the moment, you are not always going to be in a downturn. And so it just goes back to the relationship point again. If you can get the best possible recovery whilst not completely shooting your brand in the foot [...] that is pretty much the way to go.*
>
> *Senior manager, loan servicer, UK*

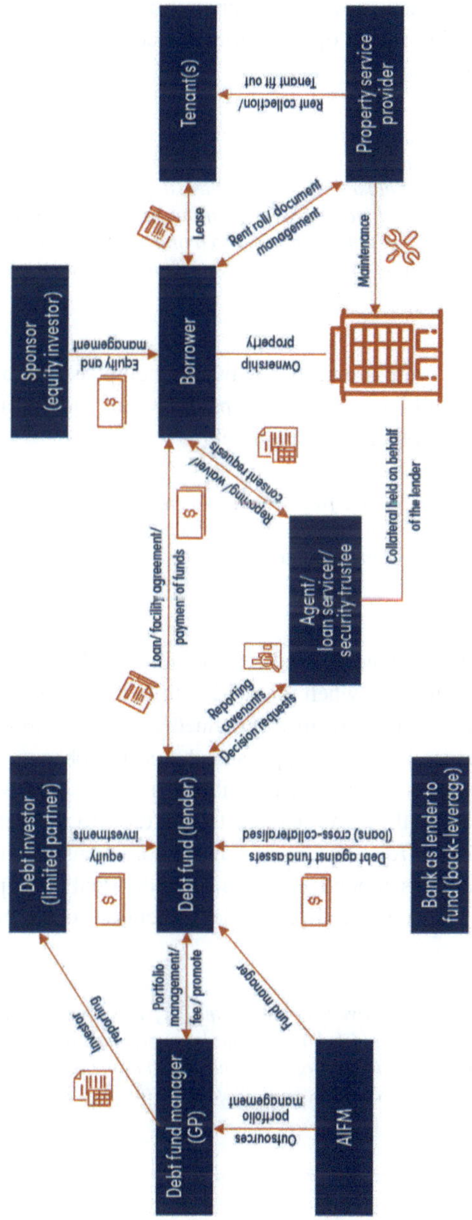

Fig. 6.3 CRE loan management—the protagonists. (Source: o. i.)

Assuming that thought and action were entrepreneurial, both parties should also have an interest in exploring future opportunities for cooperation, and thereby in generating new business.

> *It is far easier to constantly do the same deals with the same people over and over again [...] I think that the relationship aspect is something that is maybe not always thought of because you cannot close the deal and then stop [...] You are not going to start throwing things around and kicking toys out of the pram when you are trying to close the deal. So, you cannot just then flip the switch and start being very aggressive once the money is out of the door, because this is your future customer potentially.*
>
> *Senior manager, loan servicer, UK*

Nonetheless, the need for professional behaviour was emphasised, because lending relationships are usually not relationships between equals, as one party provides the funds, and the other party is in debt.

> *Alright, I am a bit prejudiced. I come from an area where relationships are becoming increasingly difficult. For me, therefore, this is a professional, distanced relationship, because I know that loans can sometimes go badly.*
>
> *Loan manager, loan servicer, Germany*

Good relations, however, provided the most favourable conditions for arriving at consensual solutions in situations when the market turned, interest rates rose, and property values collapsed, while incomes remained constant. Particularly in the UK and the US, the partnership-based approach should not obscure the fact that, unlike traditional banks, debt funds often exhibited a determined willingness to make a clean break in difficult situations and to move on to the next project. A recent significant shift from relationship-driven to more transaction-driven relations was perceived. Lenders tended to focus on individual loan performance, asking more searching questions, and paying less attention to the bigger picture of relations.

> *But I think now that the markets have become tighter [...] The positions of [non-bank lenders] are becoming trickier [...] It has become less personal, relationship-driven and these non-bank lenders are just trying to get out and manage their portfolios. And it feels like the relationship side of it has slightly gone by the wayside.*
>
> *Senior manager, borrower, UK*

The wording used by lenders and the associated connotations were of interest. While some referred to borrowers as "partners" or "counterparts", others referred to "customers" or "clients". This not only raised the question of the varied natures of lender-borrower relationships, but also the question of what the correct term would be for investors, if borrowers were referred to as customers and clients.

Regarding the maintenance of relationships between lenders and borrowers, the pros and cons of assigning third-party loan servicers were considered. Technically, a distinction is drawn between a broader understanding of the term "servicer", which includes agents, and a narrower understanding, which excludes them. This study adopted the broader understanding. Entrusted with fiduciary duties, agents acted as intermediaries between lenders and borrowers. In so doing, agents retained their roles regardless of whether lenders sold or syndicated their loans during terms. While facility agents usually took care of administrative aspects of loans, security agents held and, if necessary, enforced security interests for loan repayments on behalf of the parties. The technical and administrative roles of loan servicing, often referred to as loan surveillance, were optional. The use of third-party loan servicers appeared to be more commonplace in the UK and the US than in Germany.

While there was often no alternative to outsourcing loan surveillance for smaller debt funds with limited staff, larger debt funds apparently saw the associated cost efficiency gains conferred by outsourcing. Not only did it make sense to outsource labour-intensive administrative tasks to specialised third parties, but it was also worthwhile to benefit from their standardised procedures and broader market expertise. It should be emphasised, however, that while the administrative aspect of loan surveillance could be outsourced to intermediaries, the overall responsibility for loan risk management could not. With regard to creditor-debtor relationships, it was interesting to examine whether third parties offered their services under lenders' company names (so-called white labelling), in which case different procedures were applied. The intermediary roles of servicers were advantageous for lenders, particularly in cases where they were not comfortable having potentially relationship-damaging conversations with borrowers. The mediating position of loan servicers between the parties was, nonetheless, not always consistently adhered to.

> *There is a majority view among servicers that they are working for the lender. In fact, they should also be close to both the borrowers and [the sponsors]. Sometimes servicers make mistakes and try to push the blame onto the borrower. The loan servicer needs to realise their role is to manage both sides of the relationship equally.*
>
> *Senior manager, lender, UK*

Some lenders seemed to be concerned that by appointing third-party servicers, they would not only stand to forfeit direct interpersonal contact with borrowers, but would also jeopardise control over data and other relevant information.

> *We think that there could be a lot of important information potentially falling between the cracks when externalising services.*
>
> *Senior manager, lender, Denmark*

Usually, servicers focussed on administrative tasks and left analytics and decision-making to lenders, particularly in the event of default. Loan monitoring typically did not include the management of distressed loans, and servicers tend to be reluctant to respond in order to avoid unnecessary exposure. From the borrower's point of view, in some cases it was less burdensome to cooperate directly with an in-house loan risk management unit since the involvement of a servicer potentially added another layer of bureaucracy. From an investor's point of view, the appointment of loan servicers usually made sense for two reasons: firstly, to add another layer of protection against conflicts of interest between lenders and borrowers; and secondly, to ensure minimum levels of loan administration, in particular when dealing with non-institutional lenders.

In principle, a distinction could be drawn between institutional investors, whose investments in debt funds were equity capital, and traditional banks, which provided debt capital in so-called loan-on-loan financing, also referred to as back-leverage. From the point of view of traditional banks, debt capital that funds received was understood as corporate loans, and was therefore not considered under the more strictly regulated CRE quota. The nature of coordination and approval mechanisms depended on whether discretionary or non-discretionary investment accounts were involved. Regardless of this distinction, due diligence acquisition reviews were requested to manage actual or potential adverse impacts. In view of the prevailing market conditions, investors increasingly questioned whether debt funds had the capacity to effectively manage loan risks. There was an observable trend favouring more institutional set-ups with better integrated checks and balances.

> *As you fundraise, more and more investors ask: 'How do you manage your positions? What team do you have? What sort of systems do you have for that?' [...] Because there have been so many defaults and restructurings over the past years that it became evident to everyone that loan management is not just writing your positions and then things happen by themselves.*
>
> *Senior manager, lender, UK*

The CRE sector has thus been experiencing a sea change towards sustainability, with growing emphasis on ESG criteria. A key driver of this change has been the rise of sustainability-linked loans, which incentivise the achievement of related performance targets.

> *It makes a difference when someone is constantly breathing down your neck [...] Whether I [...] always perceive it so positively is another matter. But in terms of the facts, it is positive in any case, because you work on the issues more consistently and sustainably.*
>
> *Senior manager, borrower, Germany*

In general, investors seemed to be primarily interested in scaling their capital deployment through recurring loan investments, resembling the relationship focus found in banking businesses. The myriad uncertainties brought about by elevated interest rates, high inflation, shifts in how and where tenants occupied commercial space, and the impacts of climate change on buildings gave rise to a desire to avoid riskier investments, making it more difficult for debt funds to unlock their investment potential. As market capital became scarcer, investors acquired greater negotiating power, also with regard to their interest in and demand for effective loan risk management.

6.1.2 Loan-Level Risk Management Practices

Following the foregoing analysis of CRE debt funds' corporate structures, processes, cultures, and interorganisational relationships, the operational implementation of loan risk management is examined. After an investigation of the resources and infrastructure available at the responsible units, quantitative and qualitative measures of loan risk management are presented.

6.1.2.1 Loan Risk Management: Resources and Infrastructure

This section provides an overview of the resources and infrastructure available for loan risk management at CRE debt funds. The research areas examined included (i) the availability of qualified loan risk management staff in debt funds and the existence of suitable skill sets in the labour market; (ii) the renumeration for loan risk managers compared to that for other positions in debt funds; (iii) the reasonableness of the workload for loan risk managers; and (iv) their main areas of work. As will be shown, the percentage distribution of administrative tasks, on the one hand, and standard and non-standard management tasks, on the other, was closely related not only to the quality and degree of standardisation of reporting, but also to the availability of adequate information technologies. The influence of factors such as corporate structures and cultures on the staffing of the responsible units and the provision of efficiency-enhancing infrastructure was evident.

Among the key challenges identified was that CRE debt funds predominately employed personnel with commercial and financial skills needed for origination and underwriting, with less experience in workout, special servicing and restructuring. Particular challenges arose when staffing bottlenecks in loan risk management required temporary transfers of front office staff, who themselves had been responsible for the origination and underwriting of the loans which they would be managing. Despite these challenges, the value of working in the back office for some time before working in the front office was recognised, as it underscored risk avoidance in the initiation of new business.

The performance of loan risk management tasks required technical expertise, and skill sets in various fields, namely (i) numerical and analytical skills; (ii) financial knowledge and data affinity; (iii) real estate knowledge and understanding of capital markets; and (iv) understanding of legal aspects of loan and corporate structures, as well as of workout proceedings. While soft skills were often less appreciated in recruitment processes, they were naturally much harder to acquire on the job. These abilities included (i) people skills such as personal effectiveness, as well as interaction and intercession skills; (ii) crisis management capabilities; (iii) due diligence and attention to detail; (iv) proactiveness; (v) assertiveness towards borrowers; and (vi) the self-confidence required to present critical points in credit committees.

Knowledge transfer from and guidance by senior personnel broadened the horizons of junior staff and allowed them to absorb as much expertise as possible, and they likewise benefitted from opportunities to take part in further training, industry events, and site visits. This applied in particular to the so-called born-free generation, which had so far only experienced the boom market after the GFC.

The knowledge from workout professionals fades during the recovery times. In the next crisis, there is not sufficient staff. It is a problem that is not easy to solve as it is based on long cycles. You cannot train people for an event that is probably far in the future.

Industry expert, UK

The Royal Institution of Chartered Surveyors and the Commercial Real Estate Finance Council offer various part-time educational programmes for professionals in the real estate industry, although not specially on the topic of loan risk management.

Apart from sector-specific challenges, there were also general factors such as shortages of skilled labour caused by the so-called baby boomers retiring from the labour market with low birth cohorts following. Demographic change was affecting debt funds, which as a result of cyclical economic upswings had to expand their risk management structures in view of the increase in problematic exposures.

Renumeration was regarded as a key factor for attracting and retaining talent and highly qualified personnel. Although no exact figures were offered, it was unanimously confirmed that the renumeration of staff in back offices was generally lower than in front offices. It was pointed out that the remuneration of front office staff could be more clearly derived from business volumes, while there were no comparable indicators to measure the work performance of loan risk managers. The predominant opinion was that differences between the tasks performed by front and back office staff were sufficient grounds for salary differences.

> *Originators are key revenue drivers. If they were not finding and closing deals, asset managers would not have jobs. So, I think it is fair [that they get paid more].*
>
> *Loan manager, lender, UK*

Some respondents, however, did feel that substantial pay gaps were not justifiable.

> *You get a pat on the back when you do a new deal. Everyone is happy. Whereas in asset management [...] there is no real patting on the back for you [...] And therefore the bonuses are probably lower. Salaries are probably lower [...] You have got to originate money, but obviously you also have got to make sure it comes back to you, and that it performs as you expected. So, I think there is a disconnect.*
>
> *Loan manager, lender, UK*

The assessment of the workload adequacy of individual loan risk managers depended on the weighting of various parameters. The types and complexity of loan structures were key factors, and the same applied to the distinction between development properties and investment properties. Apart from the workload of administrative tasks, it was important to determine whether loan risk managers embarked on standard management tasks with standard credit decisions, or non-standard management tasks, for example special credit decisions on restructuring questions. Decisive factors included the percentage distribution between (i) PLs, where borrowers paid instalments as scheduled; (ii) SPLs, considered to be loans with visible or expected problems, but not yet as being in default; and (iii) NPLs, i.e. loans that were subject to significantly delayed repayments, with a high likelihood of the borrower no longer fulfilling their contractual obligations. The workload assessment also took into account whether the individuals were engaged in subordinate activities or had supervisory functions. Furthermore, consideration had to be given to whether loan servicers were contracted to support the processing and administration of loans.

As will be discussed in more detail below, the technical conditions for efficient data processing were further regarded as an important factor. Taking various factors into account, Fig. 6.4 and Fig. 6.5 illustrate the respondents' estimations regarding the workload adequacy of individual loan risk managers. The respondents qualified their answers to the question of how many loans a loan manager can typically manage with certain bandwidths with reference to the following parameters of complexity: (i) the type of loan (mezzanine versus senior loan); (ii) the type of loan structure (simple versus complicated); (iii) the type of property (development versus investment); and (iv) the risk class (value-added asset versus core asset, single asset/tenant versus multiple asset/tenants). A key variable was the support structure, i.e., whether the loan manager of a debt fund managed the loan with or without commissioning an external service provider. Somewhat beyond the main focus of this study, the loan management capacity of an external loan servicer was also explored.

Figure 6.4 shows the workload adequacy of a manager for PLs. As expected, the number of loans managed by a debt fund's loan manager was higher when assisted by an external servicer than without (10–24 loans compared to 5–10 loans, both lower to upper quartile). Limited mostly to purely administrative tasks, external loan servicers were able to manage a larger number of loans (17–30 loans). Figure 6.5 shows that a slightly different picture emerged for the management of NPLs, which required significantly more attention and effort. As external loan servicers were primarily dedicated to administrative tasks, they had less influence on the number of NPLs processed by debt fund loan managers (3–6 loans with support, compared to 3–5 without). The management capacity of external loan servicers was less influenced by the status of loans, as their involvement in risk management tasks was lower.

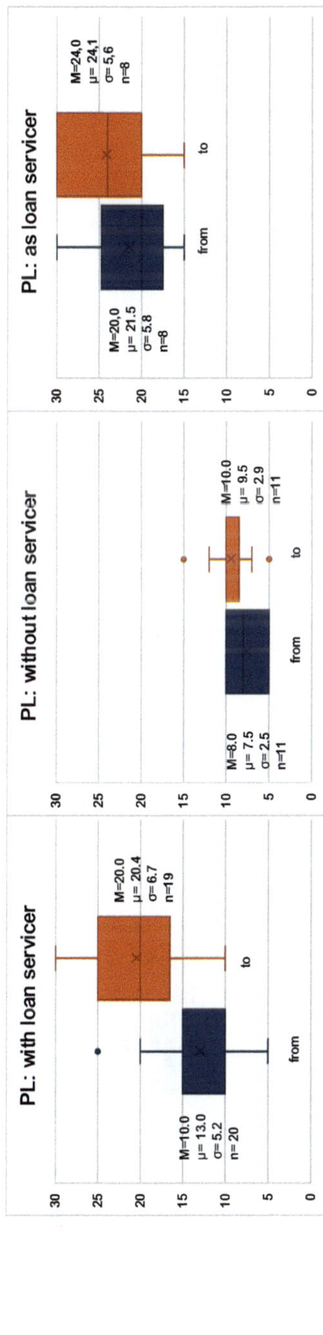

Fig. 6.4 Workload adequacy: Number of performing loans. (Source: o. i.)

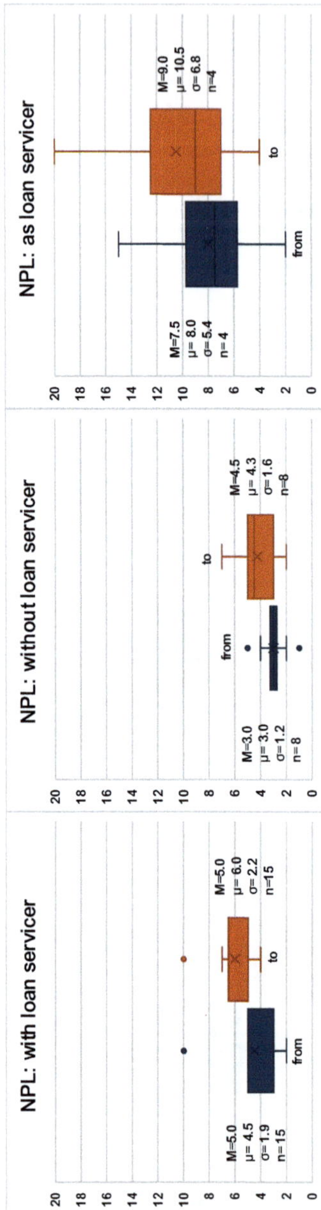

Fig. 6.5 Workload adequacy: Number of non-performing loans. (Source: o. i.)

The percentage distribution of work activities (illustrated in Fig. 6.6) also appeared to be relevant. Loan risk managers seemingly spent much of their working time on administrative activities, at the expense of standard and non-standard management tasks. Nevertheless, there were exceptions to the rule, often depending on the personnel structure of the responsible units. The effective assumption of administrative functions by loan servicers also seemed to be an important factor, as was the efficiency of data processing, to be further discussed below. With a μ of 56% and σ of 20% bandwidth approximated as in the Whisker chart (Fig. 6.6), loan managers spent between approximately 40% and 70% of their time on administrative tasks.

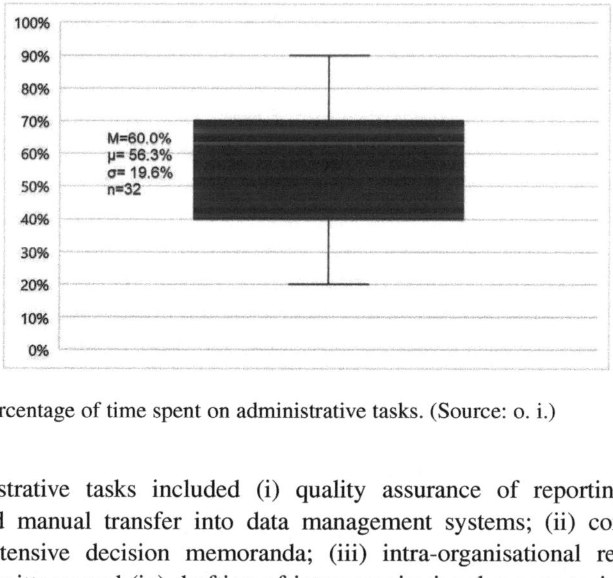

Fig. 6.6 Percentage of time spent on administrative tasks. (Source: o. i.)

Administrative tasks included (i) quality assurance of reporting by borrowers and manual transfer into data management systems; (ii) compiling of research-intensive decision memoranda; (iii) intra-organisational reporting to credit committees; and (iv) drafting of interorganisational reports to investors.

Quite often there is a whimsy from someone high up in the fund that wants to know about, you know, the number of people in the building with red trousers [...] And this cascades down and all of the sudden you find yourself doing it, and then you find yourself doing it forever [...] And it really adds no value [...] I think, yes, the answer is that there is too much time spent on admin and there is not enough time left to spend on risks.

Senior manager, loan servicer, UK

The intensity of administrative tasks certainly peaked during reporting periods. Consequently, less working time was available for standard and non-standard management tasks such as (i) stress testing and scenario analysis; (ii) watchlist analysis; (iii) market analysis of asset classes, tenants and tenants' industries (i.e. through web searches and Google news alerts); and (iv) proactive relationship management with borrowers. Although loan risk management tasks seemed to receive more attention in the prevailing cyclical downturn in the CRE market, the main point of criticism was that this attention was reactive rather than proactive.

> *Sometimes I see loan managers working on, say, a quarterly asset review. And then you say, well, when this quarterly review is done in two months or so [...] It might be too late by then. You need those quick asset reviews done within three to four weeks maximum of the interest payment date to have any impact.*
>
> *Senior manager, loan servicer, UK*

The quality and degree of standardisation of borrowers' and servicers' reporting, and the efficiency of data processing by the lender were both closely related to the limitations on the number of loans that could realistically be processed, and the respective shares of the work tasks for which they were responsible. By and large, loan risk managers at CRE debt funds worked with Excel-based systems, with data input being based on reports from borrowers and servicers. These reports were often sent by email and sometimes in PDF format, whereas Excel-based systems allowed for customised data structures that accommodated the diversity of loans. Many other currently available system designs were widely considered to be insufficiently sophisticated to handle this diversity of loans. Systems had simultaneously to meet the requirements for user-friendliness and flexibility of the front office, and for data accuracy and rigidity of the back office.

A great deal of time was expended on entering data received in Excel spreadsheets and on retrieving data for regular intra- and interorganisational reporting. As data entry and data retrieval was time-consuming, the personnel capacity for data interpretation and analysis was naturally stretched. Smaller CRE debt funds with manageable numbers of loans often did not see the need for more sophisticated information technology systems, and shied away from the costs for their development or acquisition. Excel was widely regarded as a practical and flexibly customisable tool for the management of a limited number of loans, depending on their complexity. For debt funds that already managed a significant number of loans, initially transferring data from Excel to a more advanced tool and maintaining this system involved considerable time and expense.

Regular data entry in state-of-the-art information technology tools, preferably by borrowers themselves, would require a significant degree of standardisation, which was seldom the case as a result of the diversity of reporting formats. As borrowers and loan servicers had reporting obligations for a range of lenders with differing requirements and specifications, the question also arose as to which entity had the authority to define standardised formats. As long as risk units managing significant numbers of loans were not unburdened by the provision of a state-of-the-art tool (which in turn would require the widest possible standardisation of reporting), the percentage share of work tasks was not going to change.

In cases where a large proportion of working time was spent on administrative tasks, with insufficient time being left for standard and non-standard management tasks, it was inevitable that the effectiveness of loan risk management would continue to be adversely affected. Although criticism was generally levelled at the lack of digital sophistication in this sector, the need for innovative and future-oriented approaches, such as artificial intelligence applications for rent-roll analysis, did not go unmentioned. More tech-savvy debt funds trialled existing offers, and some tinkered with their own system designs. Even if the alternative lending space seemed by and large to be relatively unimpressed by the accelerated pace of digitalisation, the realisation seemed to be gaining ground that digital transformation was required to optimise processes and enhance market competitiveness.

6.1.2.2 Quantitative Measures of Loan Risk Management

This section provides an overview on quantitative loan risk monitoring practices, namely data-driven measures. The investigation focussed on the use, usefulness and limitations of KPIs, which are frequently used numerical metrics, and of covenants, which are contractual credit conditions of lenders which borrowers must fulfil. As the distinction between KPIs and covenants is not strict or clear-cut, they are seldom separately considered and discussed. Regardless of inherent interfaces between KPIs and numerical covenants, this analysis attempted to distinguish between (i) indicators for intra-organisational risk monitoring and (ii) numerical metrics as contractually agreed parameters with borrowers, on the basis of which lenders can pursue legal action. In the event of covenant default, an important distinction exists in the way in which compliance can be enforced. While jurisdiction in the UK allows termination and enforcement of securities upon covenant defaults, Germany only allows such drastic measures upon an uncured payment default.

The most commonly used key indicators included the LTV, which is calculated based on the outstanding loan amount over the last valuation period, and the debt yield, which is the net-operating income over the outstanding loan amount. Another standard metric, the debt service cover ratio (DSCR), displays the net-operating income over the debt service amount, i.e. including interest and contractual amortisation. The interest cover ratio (ICR) shows the coverage of net-operating income over the interest amount for the relevant period. Both the ICR and the DSCR can be calculated on a backward- or forward-looking basis. Usually covering fiscal quarters, the backward-looking approach is easier to calculate, as it is based on actual historical figures. While this benefitted trend analysis, the forward-looking approach was deemed to be more relevant from a risk perspective, provided that lease extensions and expiries were given due consideration. Meanwhile, the Nordic countries proved to be early adopters when it came to the inclusion and monitoring of ESG key indicators, above all the metrics on energy performance.

The recent fall in the value of properties, which is evident in the LTV and the ICR due to the rise in net initial yields and interest rates, respectively, was highlighted as being of particular concern in the current market environment. Widely used as negotiated covenants, as will be discussed below, these standard metrics had their limitations as early warning indicators as they could be distorted by various so-called cure mechanisms. The ICR, for example, could be adjusted by reserve cash amounts, while the LTV could move independently from the income situation while the owner was in LTV breach, but the rental income remained unchanged.

> *Let me put it this way, if someone had an [early warning system] that worked [...] then we would be reading about it in the papers every day. I do not think anyone has yet found a system that can look into the future to see how the market will develop [...] If you look at how they have constantly not actually foreseen the crises [...] If this is supposed to be a bullet-proof vest, nobody would buy it because they would say: 'He already died three times, the guy.'*
>
> *Industry expert, Germany*

A distinction must therefore also be drawn between purely numerical KPIs and additional early warning signs that cannot be expressed in exclusively quantitative terms. The latter included performance-related indicators, such as (i) variable interest rates and resulting interest payment risks affecting borrowers; (ii) tenant payment arrears; (iii) impacts of imminent breaks on lease terms and, consequently, the weighted average lease term; (iv) rising vacancy rates; (v) capital expenditure (CapEx) backlogs, combined with poor appearances of properties; and (vi) unpaid subcontractor invoices in the case of development projects.

We were looking at one [building] recently that was described as a performing loan with some CapEx on it. When you actually looked at it, you saw that this was a tired 1990s building that actually needed quite a lot of CapEx spending on it. And the void periods are getting longer, and the WALT are getting shorter, and the rent is staying flat. And by the time you worked out and you looked at the things together, it was just like, this is a building in trouble […] If you put your pessimist hat on, I think you are definitely able to see things that have the potential to be going in the wrong direction. Before it is obvious that they are going in the wrong direction.

Senior manager, loan servicer, UK

Other early warning signs of distress could be rather behaviour-related, including (i) payments by borrowers overdue at interest payment dates; (ii) consistent delays and missed deadlines in borrowers' reporting; (iii) inaccurate reporting with striking number deviations and unexplained costs; and (iv) unanswered emails or calls, in some cases leading to breakdowns in direct communication.

Effective risk management should focus on monitoring two types of risks: (i) factored-in structural risks inherent in certain asset classes, geographic regions and capital structures; and (ii) often underweighted cyclical risks to be determined through a holistic combination of KPI monitoring and covenant testing, with observation and foresight of external market conditions. Google news alerts were deemed to be useful to forecast the economic performance of borrowers, of tenants in trouble but not yet in default on rental payments, and, consequently, of anticipated reductions in lease levels and asset values.

The capacity to manage this data and generate insights requires investment, and the willingness to pay for these insights might be limited. However, identifying issues three months earlier [rather] than a year later or more could significantly impact the ability to change behaviours or to make early interventions, potentially saving a lot of money, reducing risks, and seizing opportunities.

Industry expert, UK

Certain challenges arose from the information asymmetry between lenders and borrowers. Other challenges arose from the often purely administrative, sometimes even selective third-party monitoring executed by loan servicers. The raw data provided by borrowers and loan servicers should be used by lenders for the evaluation of future scenarios, analysis of cash flow and trends in projected rental income, forecasts based on borrowers and anchor tenants profiles, and understanding of the effects of macroeconomic events. However, whether most debt funds actually did this was called into question.

> *In good times, you simply have to check tenant lists. Perhaps an external [servicer] can do this. But what do you do if the tenant list does not arrive? How do you find out what is going on with the sponsor? How do you find out from the newspaper that the sponsor has someone on the supervisory board who has a criminal record for money laundering? [...] Even if the asset is running smoothly, you should check everything. That is risk management. And how you want to do that through [an external servicer] is beyond me when it comes to debt funds [...] You get an information mismatch that you simply cannot afford.*
>
> *Senior manager, lender, Germany*

Furthermore, smaller debt funds often did not have the necessary variety of data needed for comparative interpretation on the basis of benchmarks. Even though ostensibly reasonable from a cost-saving perspective, the criticism was also levelled that PLs usually received less attention than SPLs on the watchlist or NPLs in special servicing. The comparison could be made with a healthcare system that shies away from incurring costs for prevention and early detection, without adequately taking into account the costs incurred for the treatment of diseases when they do occur.

> *Yes, obviously these loans in distress need more focus, but what element of that could have been dealt with if it had more attention at an earlier stage? Should it really be that a performing [loan] gets very little attention, and it progresses as it deteriorates, it gets more attention? Or could you actually have staved off some of the concerns and addressed it and actually delivered a better result by paying closer attention earlier in the process?*
>
> *Loan manager, lender, UK*

Unlike KPIs used for internal risk monitoring, contractually agreed covenants serve the purpose of acting as legal trigger mechanisms. Providing intersections with quantitative KPIs, numerical covenants contain key figures. The LTV, debt yield, ICR and DSCR were frequently used as standard metrics. Often referred to as information covenants, qualitative covenants related to the provision of information on agreed undertakings, such as the conclusion of insurance policies. Furthermore, hard covenants, which included loan termination options, were distinguished from soft covenants, which served as contractual alarm bells and could activate penalty mechanisms against the borrower, e.g. cash sweeps or cash traps.

Covenants were thus often intensely negotiated, firstly, to avoid any ambiguity, and secondly, to give the borrower sufficient headroom before activation. Consequently, covenants tended to be triggered at rather late stages, and thus seldom qualified as effective early warning parameters. Caution thus dictates that one should distinguish between covenants as purely legal trigger mechanisms, on the one hand, and the monitoring of a wider set of parameters that could more effectively function as early warning mechanisms, on the other.

> *Well, I think a lot of covenants are historic tests that could potentially be slightly manipulated by sponsors, intentionally or unintentionally.*
>
> *Loan manager, lender, UK*

A general observation regarding CRE lending was that once a hard covenant default had occurred, the deterioration in value had often already reached a point where a lender could no longer assume that a hard enforcement of the security, i.e. sale of the property, would cover the outstanding loan amount.

> *Your covenants are almost the breaks before you hit the wall [...] What you want is a controlled stop. Ideally. But there are a lot of people that seem to be driving the car while looking at where they have just been out the back window, instead of looking forwards.*
>
> *Senior manager, loan servicer, UK*

Considering the legal costs involved, the human resources required, and the potential discount to be expected from a so-called fire sale, it was by no means certain that recoveries would pay off the lender. Consequently, it frequently occurred that lenders would shy away from hard enforcement and be unwilling, as the saying goes, to "put their money where their mouth is". Instead, they often sought a more consensual route with the borrower.

As will be further discussed in the following section, effective loan risk management required two well-balanced and integrated functional roles: data analysis, and human interaction. Anecdotal evidence suggested that the combination of both talents in a single staff member responsible for loan risk management was rare. Regular personal dialogue between lenders and borrowers was, however, widely understood to be the most effective means of understanding the context, before numbers triggered red flags.

6.1.2.3 Qualitative Measures of Loan Risk Management

This section outlines which qualitative measures relating to loan risk monitoring practices were observed at CRE debt funds. In this study, qualitative measures are understood as reviews of borrowers' and service providers' reporting, and regular internal valuations of the quality and desirability of properties. As the supervision of risk management processes in the purview of borrowers and loan servicers was among the core tasks of the responsible units, numerous interorganisational interfaces were involved. Lastly, the types, potentials and limitations of externally commissioned property valuations are examined in order to map all key processes relevant to loan risk management.

Borrower reporting usually took place on a quarterly basis for investment properties, and on a monthly basis for development properties. These fairly standard reporting cycles mainly applied to so-called plain vanilla loans. Reporting frequency naturally increased as performance deteriorated, with weekly or even daily reporting frequencies in cases of loans on the watchlist or in special servicing. The realisation of this common approach proved to be problematic when the reins had been left too loose over long periods, in particular in crisis situations, when historical data were sought but could no longer be obtained.

> *Make sure that [borrowers] provide [the information], every single part of it. Because I have seen it countless times that information is missing. But that did not seem massively important in the first couple of quarters. But when it comes to the deal starting to teeter a bit, and you are looking down the line [...] it is far more difficult to get the information because you never asked for it before [...] And so if we are not getting this information from the borrower in the first place, we cannot really do our jobs optimally.*
>
> *Senior manager, loan servicer, UK*

Debt funds received borrowers' reports directly or via intermediary third-party loan servicers, with the latter approach seeming to have been more prevalent in the UK than in Germany. It was argued that the outsourcing of loan servicing might create certain information mismatches that could no longer be tolerated when markets became tighter, and positions became trickier.

Regarding the timeliness of reporting, a range of behaviours from borrowers could be observed, with significantly late reporting often interpreted as a red flag for the status of a property. The general lack of standardised reporting formats was highlighted as a challenge, as it compromised the comparability of data which would have allowed the monitoring of trends, both over time and between loans. In some cases, borrower reports were guided by the legal requirements of the facility agreement provided by the Loan Market Association, which, however, was criticised as having the character of a so-called laundry list. Other debt funds developed their own reporting templates that allowed for flexible application to various asset classes, such as hotels, student accommodation, office space, and build-to-rent properties. Various strategies were used to persuade borrowers to apply standard formats designed by lenders. Some promoted the idea of offering discounts to borrowers who complied with their reporting requirements. Others included clauses in loan agreements that allowed them to appoint third-party experts to provide quality assurance of reports at the borrowers' expense. There seemed to be agreement that it was preferable to define reporting requirements in loan agreements at the outset, and to consistently monitor compliance.

A relevant correlation emerged between reporting quality and borrower type, relating to the degree of institutionalisation or location. For example, it was argued that varying compliance with reporting requirements could be attributed to the different legal frameworks in the UK and Germany. While in the UK, any default could be legally enforced, including covenant default, German law limited this option to payment default. Some argued that larger institutional borrowers submitted better quality reports because they had established organisational structures with dedicated personnel, while smaller debt funds, such as family offices, required more handholding. Referring to the balance of power between lenders and borrowers, others argued that larger institutional borrowers could not be dictated to, while smaller borrowers had to be more flexible and adaptable.

> *It is a disaster. It is a disaster. Always. And people tend to say: 'Because it is [name of larger borrower], the reporting must be good. And when you go with smaller borrowers, the reporting is not so good.' It is not true. The problem with the bigger borrower is that they have a lot of power of negotiation. They will often say to the lenders: 'This is what you are getting. Do not get annoyed with me. Otherwise, I am going and get funding from somebody else, and you are going to lose on this big deal.' […] It very much comes down to negotiation power between the two.*
>
> *Senior manager, lender, UK*

There was broad consensus that personal meetings between lenders and borrowers were necessary and beneficial. Face-to-face meetings took place either in the respective offices or on site. There was also wide agreement on the required frequency of these meetings, including the determining factors. Annual or bi-annual strategy and budget meetings were by and large deemed to be sufficient for PLs on investment properties. For development properties, lenders literally had to put their boots on the ground more frequently, preferably on a monthly or bi-monthly basis. More frequent meetings and site visits became necessary when borrowers were in breach of covenants, signs of distress became apparent, and loans were placed on watchlists. These meetings were not necessarily unilaterally initiated by lenders. Borrowers also showed an interest in understanding lenders' moods and, in cases of loan default, discussing the commission of lawyers and restructuring experts.

In addition to face-to-face meetings, there were also exchanges via video conference, telephone, or email. Online communication naturally played a greater role when lenders and borrowers were in widely separated locations, possibly even in different countries. Calls were often scheduled around the time of quarterly report submission, in particular when an issue was flagged in the early warning system.

> *I think human behaviour is a massively underutilised tool. [It is important] to really understand peoples' businesses, and how they work, and what they are excited about for the future, and what they are nervous about.*
>
> *Loan manager, lender, UK*

There were differences between which modes of communication were favoured, apparently also due to generation gaps between senior and junior personnel. Some senior staff were unequivocal in their support for in-person and telephonic conversations, and rated video conferencing and, above all, email exchanges as less effective.

> *This is the discussion I have quite often with my younger staff members. Then, I say: 'Ok Mr. X, have you spoken to this person?' And he says: 'Yes, I have'. And I say: 'Have you really spoken to this person, or did you write an email?' Then, he says: 'No, I wrote an email.' That is not the same thing. If you write an email to a person that is of my age, it has no effect. But if you call me and you really talk to me, that has a different effect. And I think if you need to have a tough discussion or if you need to penetrate the debate, you need to ask on a deeper level. You need to call the person. You cannot just send an email.*
>
> *Senior manager, lender, Sweden*

The value of fostering sustainable and future-oriented relationships between lenders and borrowers was emphasised. Regular meetings should be set up not just for one-way reporting but instead as opportunities for mutually beneficial exchange. Beyond reporting on specific loans, the added value of the discussions would also lie in exchanges on market trends and their impacts on the business sector, including threats and opportunities. Beyond the current engagements, maintaining relationships between lenders and borrowers served the purpose of jointly identifying new business opportunities for future transactions.

Mention should also be made of the fact that property valuations should ideally be commissioned from external experts about once a year to provide independent perspectives. There were indications that these valuations were requested more frequently in the UK and the US than in the German context. Various methods are typically applied to value commercial real estate properties, including: (i) the cost approach, which looks at the value of the land and then adds the replacement cost of the building; (ii) the sales comparison approach, which uses recent property sales information to estimate the value of unsold assets; and (iii) the income approach, which estimates the value of a property based on the income it generates. Other commercial real estate valuation approaches include (iv) the residual method, which calculates the value of the land/site by using a hypothetical development estimating a future sale price and then deducting construction and planning costs, financing costs, transaction costs and profits; and finally, (v) various advanced regression methods, neural networks, and hedonic or spatial models (Pagourtzi et al., 2003) that can be utilised. A common characteristic of these valuation methods is that they predominantly use comparable transactions to determine property values. In times of weak markets with low trading volumes, this primarily backward-looking perspective of external property valuations naturally limited their usefulness for foresighted loan risk management.

6.1.3 Concluding Remarks

In the following, key findings are presented, summarising responses to research questions addressed in subchapter 6.1.

Taking into account the diversity of debt fund corporate structures, interrelationships between fund sizes and the endowment of effective loan risk management were confirmed. While institutional funds with appropriate processes also showed certain imbalances in staffing between back and front offices, they usually had the capital and structures to fall back on, in contrast to smaller funds and those in the development phase. A functional separation of asset management and risk management was not always in place, and in some cases where it was in place, credit risk officers were assigned to back offices, whereas cross-departmental positioning could be observed in others.

Debt funds typically went through four successive loan phases, with key determinants being integrated or segregated procedures between front and back offices, and the assignment or non-assignment of third-party loan servicers. The extent to which loan risk managers were involved in background checks at early stages of investment review processes depended on available resources, and whether transaction approaches were more relationship-driven or transaction-driven. Whether risk managers were involved in the underwriting phase to mitigate the often-present deal bias and to share learning experiences from previously administered loan portfolios was handled in differing ways. There were also different schools of thought on outsourcing loan surveillance and administration to intermediaries, with those decisions to some extent but not exclusively being determined by funds' loan ticket sizes and staffing levels. It was not only a company's headcount, but also its philosophy that determined whether and to what extent interaction with borrowers was handed over by originators during the loan management phase. The information provided by borrowers and servicers was administratively processed, reviewed and analysed, and then presented to investment committees. Either debt recurred in the ordinary course of business as per contractual obligations, or payment default occurred and restructuring proceedings were initiated.

Anecdotal evidence suggested that corporate cultures determined attitudes and behaviours towards loan risk management. As competition for loan acquisition was high and margins comparatively low, the focus was on front offices as capital-raising value drivers, while back offices were widely perceived as cost centres. Disaster myopia was observed, combined with a tendency to countenance investments even in the face of adverse evidence. Despite high requirements for technical and soft skills, the role of loan risk management seemed to be widely underappreciated, as was reflected in significant remuneration gaps between back and front offices.

Both lenders and borrowers showed interest in maintaining good relations and transparent communication, not only to explore future business opportunities, but also to create the best conditions for consensual solutions in the event of a loan default. In response to rising loan default rates, however, a shift from relationship-driven to more transaction-driven relations could be observed. Arguments were made in support of appointing loan servicers, based on cost efficiency gains, the availability of specialist personnel, and the application of standardised procedures. Negative arguments related in particular to a lack of personal contact between lenders and borrowers and the potential for loss of control over data and information. As market capital became scarcer, investors acquired increased bargaining power, and their negotiating positions thus enabled them to enforce demands for effective credit risk management.

Regarding staff qualifications at debt funds, commercial and financial skills tended to be in higher demand than the specific technical expertise and soft skills needed for loan risk management. The workload adequacy of loan risk managers depended on various parameters of complexity, such as loan types, loan structure, and both property and risk class. Whether an external servicer was commissioned was another key variable, influencing not only workload adequacy but also the percentage distribution of tasks. Both workload adequacy and percentage distribution of tasks were also closely related to the quality and degree of standardisation of borrowers' and servicers' reporting, and the efficiency of data processing by lenders. Despite widespread criticism of the sector's digital underdevelopment, there were some innovative approaches promising digital process optimisation.

As contractually agreed parameters, KPIs predominantly use numerical standard metrics, as do covenants. Differentiation was evident between purely numerical metrics and other performance- and behaviour-related indicators which could not be expressed in exclusively quantitative terms. A distinction must also be made between hard covenants with termination options, and soft covenants, which just served as contractual alarm bells. As covenants often only got triggered at fairly late stages, their value as early warning parameters was limited.

Borrowers' reporting was either direct or via intermediary loan servicers. Typically, the largely standardised reporting frequency depended on the performance status of the loan. While a range of behaviours was observed regarding the timeliness of reporting, there were correlations between reporting quality and borrower type, and it is quite possible that compliance with requirements was influenced by the differing legal frameworks of Germany and the UK. Whilst there was broad consensus on the benefits of personal meetings between lenders and borrowers, there were differences in which modes of communication were favoured. Although regular external property valuations provided independent perspectives, due to their backward-looking methods, their usefulness for forward-looking loan risk management was limited.

With their focus on loan risk management practices in the alternative lending space, these research findings address the broad knowledge gap identified in peer-reviewed academic research. Considering both the organisational lender level and the operational loan level, this study provides long overdue insights into the loan risk management practices of debt funds. The research was solely focussed on the commercial property industry, which had hitherto been underrepresented in academic publications. This was true in particular of peer-reviewed literature with a European focus, which had been far outweighed by US-specific studies. Above all, this study shone a spotlight on debt funds in the alternative lending space, which with their growing market share had become an essential feature of the CRE sector, but had so far not attracted the academic interest they deserve.

Consequently, with its focus on the alternative lending space that had been under-researched for far too long, this research complemented and broadened the scope of bank-specific academic writings.

6.2 Effects of Risk Management Practices on Loan Performance

Following the examination and assessment of the loan risk management practices of CRE debt funds, this subchapter responds to the second core dimension of the two-staged central research question: What were the plausible effects of these practices on loan performance? While bearing the strong likelihood of multicausality in mind, the aim was to test whether loan risk management had a significant impact on loan performance, and also to identify contextual factors that could be assumed to have been influential in this regard. As illustrated by the systematic ex-ante impact model, it was assumed that there were interrelationships between the loan risk monitoring of CRE debt funds and intervening external factors, which crossed system boundaries. As explained, it should be among the key tasks of the units entrusted with loan risk management not only to identify risks, but also to assess their observed and anticipated impacts on loans, and to estimate lenders' and borrowers' abilities to influence and mitigate those risks. This subchapter is introduced by an overview on key success factors for effective loan risk management and ends with brief concluding remarks.

6.2.1 Key Success Factors for Effective Loan Risk Management

Key success factors are decisive criteria and influencing variables that were deemed to be critical for the effectiveness of the loan risk management of CRE debt funds. As will be shown, this effectiveness depended on various interlinked and mutually dependent organisational and operational factors. This representation of key success factors was largely based on convincing evidence of best-practices, gathered through the experience of experts and conveyed in their responses. Consequently, this presentation of the key success factors is based on the structure and contents of the previous chapter on the loan risk management practices of CRE debt funds.

Corporate structures:

- The functional separation between origination and loan asset management, and preferably also between origination and underwriting, was widely considered to be a requirement not only for unbiased loan management, but also for ensuring that the responsible personnel had the technical expertise and soft skills that they required.
- Insofar as feasible for debt funds given their respective loan ticket sizes, back offices should be adequately staffed, even during real estate market upswings.
- The functional separation between loan asset management and risk management was regarded as preferable and where feasible, independent cross-departmental credit risk officers endowed with veto rights should be appointed.

Corporate processes:

- Ideally, credit risk officers should be involved in background checks at early stages of investment review processes. To ensure that financial allocations were made to companies regarded as trustworthy, not only should properties be valued during the origination phase, but the creditworthiness of borrowers should also be assessed. Credit analysis processes should not only focus on the creditworthiness of borrowers and current property values, but should also consider potential losses arising from non-performance and bad debt.
- The early involvement of loan risk managers could not only mitigate frequently occurring deal bias, but could also broaden the decision-making basis by including lessons learnt from administered loan portfolios.
- There were different schools of thought regarding the further involvement of originators in interaction with borrowers during the asset management phase. Second-tier or subordinate roles for front offices in relation to back offices were, in any case, identified as best practice.
- Operational and strategic credit decisions should optimally be systematically assigned to different levels of corporate hierarchies, with the use of decision-making matrices for approvals.

Corporate cultures:

- Corporate resilience requires not only profit maximisation but also the minimisation of losses. Recognising this demands a willingness to view investing in apparently non-revenue generating units from a new perspective, as cost savings in this area have the potential to backfire in the event of loan default.

Various options were presented on how loan risk management units could better demonstrate performance-related returns.

- Driven by the economic downturn, there was increasing recognition of the importance of the loan risk management function. This could change how it is perceived, and thereby enable debt funds to better attract and retain talent.

Interorganisational relationships:

- Trust-based relationships between lenders and borrowers, founded on mutual respect, readiness to compromise, and open communication, provide the best conditions for consensual solutions in the event of loan default. Professional interaction should, however, be maintained, especially in relationship-driven transactions with prospects of generating new business.
- It was essential to distinguish between the administrative aspects of loans, which might be undertaken by external third-party servicers, and the internal governance task of loan risk management, for which authority should not (and responsibility cannot) be delegated to intermediaries.

Resources and infrastructure:

- Not only the technical expertise required for loan risk management, but also relevant soft skills should be factored into recruitment processes. Staff from the so-called born-free generation should be familiarised with the challenges of economic downturns through market exposure and guidance from experienced senior personnel.
- The availability of appropriate information technology and, thus, the efficiency of data processing were considered to be key factors for both workload adequacy and the equitable percentage distribution of work activities of loan risk managers. A precondition for the efficient use of state-of-the-art tools would be the widest possible standardisation of borrowers' and servicers reporting. Effective loan risk management required staff members to spend more of their working hours on standard and non-standard management tasks, and fewer on purely administrative tasks.

Quantitative measures:

- Complementing purely numerical standard metrics, performance- and behaviour-related indicators have proven to be significant early warning signals.

- Early mitigation measures have the potential to significantly assist in reaching consensual solutions, thereby reducing the impact of risks on loan performance, saving on expenses incurred on restructuring experts and legal advisors, and enabling the seizing of opportunities for new business with counterparts.

Qualitative measures:

- Effective loan risk management required both data analysis and human interaction. Regular personal dialogue between lenders and borrowers was, thus, widely understood to be the most effective means of understanding the context, before numbers raised red flags. There was broad consensus that both frequent personal meetings between lenders and borrowers and regular site visits at investment and development properties were indispensable.
- Various strategies were used to persuade borrowers to apply standard reporting formats. Broad standardisation was not only a prerequisite for efficient digitalisation, but it also allowed lenders to better monitor trends. With regard to reporting standards, the reins should not be left too loose for too long, as in crises situations, it can be more difficult to access historical data.

Additional considerations on effective loan risk management are now presented, complementing the key success factors that emerged from the practical experience shared by respondents. Internal risk factors should be distinguished from external risk factors, with the former relating to debt funds' own structures and processes, and the latter to contextual factors that are more difficult to influence. Internal risks could be avoided by appropriate management; the threats posed by external risks, however, could typically not be entirely avoided, but their impacts on loan performance could be mitigated, albeit to varying degrees. Furthermore, a distinction should be drawn between observed and anticipated risks, with the probability of occurrence to be estimated for the latter. An assessment should be made not only of the severity of the potential impacts of these risks on loan performance, i.e. expected losses, but also of the ability of lenders and borrowers to mitigate these impacts. Mitigation measures should be identified, recommended and implemented, and their effectiveness should furthermore also be assessed through follow-up reviews. For the sake of completeness, it should be emphasised once again that risk management should be an ongoing task that extends beyond the underwriting phase in which risks are initially assessed and conditions for loans determined.

As will be discussed in the following chapter, effective loan risk management practices are shown to have positively impacted the performance of loans. Evidence shows that the positive effects were significantly enhanced when these practices were aligned with the listed key success factors.

6.2.2 Exploration of the Cause-Effect Relationship

In this section, evidence is presented that plausibly confirms the causal mechanisms between the loan risk management practices of debt funds and loan performance. This section draws substantially on the decisive criteria and influencing variables for effective loan management, and arrives at pertinent conclusions regarding the exploration of this cause-effect relationship. The term "effect" was defined as an outcome caused by specific factors, and positive effects were distinguished from negative ones.

First, the positive influence of effective loan risk management on loan performance is explored. For this purpose, core statements of experts who were asked what debt funds need to do to get ahead of the curve were analysed. Whilst tailored to the specific research focus of this study, this analysis drew on Harold Leavitt's diamond model (Leavitt, 1965), which was introduced in the mid-1960s to guide organisational change processes. The original diamond model considered four elements: structures, tasks, people, and technologies. Structures and tasks could also be grouped together as processes. For the purposes of this study, the element "people" was applied to both personnel structures and relationships.

Critical factors that determined positive causal effects between loan risk management practices and loan performance are presented along the lines of these elements. As there were naturally interrelations and intersections between the elements, they could not be altogether independently categorised. While there seemed to be general consensus on what the key factors were, respondents did not always agree on how they should be ranked for relevance. Although there were more similarities than differences, experts relied on differing key strategies to mitigate the impact of distressed loans and minimise losses.

Checks and balances between the functional units in decision-making processes were identified as a key factor. The most critical strategy in minimising losses through distressed deals was to prevent debt funds from entering into potentially loss-making deals in the first place. In retrospect, it might be argued that the impact of the recent global crises on the commercial property market could not have been predicted, and that office buildings on the outskirts of cities were still considered to be promising investments shortly before the outbreak of the Covid-19 pandemic. The strategy, however, should have been to exploit the potential of the best critical, independent expertise, which could have counteracted the deal bias that is often seen among origination teams and senior managements.

> *Obviously, the main regret a lender has when a situation turns sour is wishing they had never made the loan rather than managed it differently.*
>
> *Industry expert, UK*

Exemplary decision-making frameworks provided for the involvement of loan risk officers in credit analysis and credit structuring processes, ideally vested with veto rights. This allowed for the early evaluation of stress scenarios and the identification of downside risks. For smaller debt funds that lacked the team size to divide responsibilities so that employees could focus on different risk viewpoints, making use of external directors could mitigate this limitation.

> *You can be the greatest loan manager in the world, but if somebody writes a bad deal and the underwriting is poorly, there is absolutely nothing you can do. A bad deal is a bad deal from the second it is signed.*
>
> *Senior manager, loan servicer, UK*

These control mechanisms should ideally be entrenched in the loan management phase by maintaining an adequate functional separation between origination and asset management. It is to be expected that people who have advocated and promoted deals might often find it difficult to critically examine their own reasoning in retrospect.

Proactiveness and timeliness were identified as further key points. Proactiveness was one of the buzzwords most frequently mentioned in expert interviews. Systematic and robust approaches to loan management allowed debt funds to act early on warning signals and to mitigate distressed situations before they escalated.

> *Spotting problems early. The earlier you spot problems, the easier it is to fix them because you have the benefit of time.*
>
> *Senior manager, lender, UK*

Without doubt, not being taken by surprise, but rather reacting the moment trouble appears on the horizon would be the most effective strategy to resolve issues before reaching loan default.

We are sitting on our hands too long [...] We should have looked at alternative solutions early, at an earlier stage. We were not really keen on looking at the early warning signs, asking 'Okay, do we really do something now? Should we speak about solutions already now? Or wait just another quarter until it happens?'

Senior manager, lender, Denmark

The early detection of potentially distressed situations would not be sufficient on its own, however, as it was also deemed to be crucial for senior management to swiftly implement the appropriate decision-making processes.

The decisions themselves probably come early, it is just that they are not consistent [...] The hope factor is overemphasised because [lenders] do not want to tell their investors that they have issues [...] However, it is also human because people do not want to deliver negative messages.

Senior manager, loan servicer, Germany

It was emphasised that decisive approaches required courage and a willingness to shoulder responsibility, as merely hoping for better times would all too often have been the easier route.

Of course, you also have to be brave. Suppose, for example, when Ukraine was invaded [...] The really brave asset managers get into situations early on, where there is no default yet and no major signs of it either. You have to decide early on: I am getting out of the position. And that costs a lot of money at the beginning, and you need good arguments against the doubters [...] Not that I would do that, I am probably a wimp too [...] But the really successful ones do that [...] They recognise trends early, implement [measures] and take the losses early. And these losses are often not quite as harsh.

Senior manager, loan servicer, Germany

Nonetheless, the benefit of early responses in some situations does not justify drastic measures being taken too early. Prudence and careful consideration should not be sacrificed in order to rush into action. Accurately assessing the likelihood of improvement or deterioration in situations often required a difficult balancing act.

In view of the dynamics of property markets, recovering investments while not compromising relationships and future business opportunities with borrowers was also referred to as a tightrope walk. Good lender-borrower relationships assumed that the parties were both motived by a shared economic interest in avoiding bankruptcies.

> *I have seen cases where a good relationship directly influenced the outcome of a situation, where there was a breach or a near breach [...] Having a good relationship with the borrower helped us all reach a solution quicker, and that benefits everyone.*
>
> *Loan manager, lender, UK*

Nevertheless, sharing a roughly similar understanding of a property's value would be prerequisite for finding a mutually acceptable solution.

> *The most important success factor is a common understanding that everyone can agree [on]. Everyone must have the same parameters in mind: the investment value, the difficulties and the goal [...] If one person thinks that the value of the property is 100 million and the other believes it is worth nothing, then there is no common ground.*
>
> *Loan manager, loan servicer, Germany*

Finally, suitably qualified staff and modern information technology were identified as basic requirements for loan risk management to positively affect loan performance. It was widely acknowledged that efficiency gains provided by cutting-edge information technology enabled qualified personnel to reduce the administrative burden and to focus on value-generating loan management tasks. However, a certain lack of willingness to invest in advanced systems and pay for the insights they provided was observed. Hybrid systems involving both external loan servicing and internal loan management represented a compromise, which could be successful as long as there was a clear understanding of the respective roles and responsibilities.

Just as effective loan risk management practices positively influenced loan performance, less effective procedures had adverse impacts. These inverse effects can be compared with a photographic negative, in which light appears as dark, and vice versa. For the sake of simplicity and to avoid repetition, only a brief summary of the loan management pitfalls which have the potential to negatively affect loan performance is given. These are: (i) insufficient checks and balances due to inadequate functional separation of operational units; (ii) the lack of involvement of credit risk managers in investment review processes and the underwriting phase, and thus insufficient consideration of lessons learnt from administered loan portfolios; (iii) inefficient and ineffective decision-making processes that were not systematically assigned to different levels of the corporate hierarchy;

(iv) a lack of awareness that minimising losses is just as important as maximising profits; (v) inadequate corporate appreciation of back office staff, often manifested in income disparities, lack of recognition of the required qualifications, and consequently, high staff turnover; (vi) the lack of proactive, transparent and timely lender-borrower communication; and (vii) the lack of standardised borrower reporting and of modern information technology, resulting in the overburdening of loan risk managers with administrative activities, at the expense of standard and non-standard management tasks.

As will be argued in the next section, there were no monocausal relationships between loan risk management practices and loan performance. There were also no mechanisms that guaranteed that good practices would always lead to satisfactory results, or that workout and restructuring processes, even if successful, would not prove to be time-consuming and costly. The conclusion to be drawn, instead, was that optimised structures and processes were basic requirements for achieving the best possible outcomes. The analogy of a cruise ship comes to mind: in good weather, lifeboats seem almost expendable; in stormy weather, there is also no guarantee that all crew members and passengers will reach the lifeboats in time, and that there will be no loss of life. Nevertheless, having enough lifeboats on board and holding regular safety drills provide the best possible conditions for ensuring the survival of passengers and crew members.

6.2.3 Contributing and Interfering External Factors

In this section, loan risk management's contribution to loan performance is ranked in comparison with other contributing and interfering external factors. The contribution claim of loan risk management should not be understood as being independent from other influencing factors. Indeed, interrelationships between loan risk monitoring of CRE debt funds and other factors were observed. The key functions of loan risk management should include not just the identification of market risks, but also an assessment of their observed and anticipated impacts on loans, and an estimation of lenders' and borrowers' ability to mitigate those risks. This section therefore addresses the second-tier questions of whether external interfering factors directly and indirectly influenced loan performance, and if they did, in what way they did so.

The first and most significant external influencing factor which had direct and indirect effects on the performance of loans was the economic cycle. The CRE cycle generally follows a sequence of recovery, expansion, hyper-supply, and recession (ESRB, 2019a). During the expansion phase, the real estate market experiences an upswing seen in increased demand, rising property prices, and dropping vacancy rates (ESRB, 2015). Market circumstances are deemed to be generally favourable, and it is an excellent time to acquire and hold properties. Before the series of global crises that significantly impacted the real estate capital markets, there had been such a long phase of expansion that most lenders, borrowers and investors had little institutional experience of significant downturns. Following the guiding principle of "no deal is no option" in a highly competitive market environment, debt funds found themselves to be increasingly under pressure to identify investment opportunities in order to deploy capital that was being eagerly provided by investors. In Europe, the deal bias of debt funds was also driven by investors' invested capital fee approach. This was largely different from the US, where the prevailing fee on committed capital allowed debt funds to take breather breaks. Seemingly not anticipating market disruptions, regulatory bodies adopted a fairly hands-off approach towards CRE debt funds (Bank for International Settlements, 2023; Bank of England, 2024a; ESRB, 2024), which in view of the prosperous real estate market at the time had little incentive to invest in their loan risk management structures.

> *A bad loan is made in a good market. The same applies to a bad investment.*
>
> *Senior management, lender, UK*

Despite the persistent and apparently resilient market boom, there were early signs of a real estate bubble developing (DeNederlanscheBank, 2019; ECB, 2020). The ever-widening gap between property values and their earning capacity already warned of the risk of devaluation. The commercial real estate crisis had its harbinger in the rapid and continued increase in e-commerce, coupled with a decrease in demand for retail space. The lockdowns widely imposed as public health responses during the Covid-19 pandemic had accelerated this trend in customer behaviour. After the pandemic, working from home, at least on some weekdays, continued to be the norm in many sectors of the economy. Office vacancy rates increased, and the value of office space eroded.

> *Unfortunately, crises happen again and again [...] CRE loans were treated as safe investments, but that was not the case. The ECB's interest rate hike was foreseeable. It was clear that the zero interest rate environment would not last forever and that at some point we would have to expect interest rates to normalise. There was certainly negligence here. What was unforeseeable from my point of view was the transformation of the workplace, triggered by Covid. This was a shock that severely disrupted the real estate market.*

Industry expert, Germany

Russia's war of aggression against Ukraine was considered to be the final trigger that brought on the CRE crisis. The series of supply bottlenecks in the real economy, particularly of building materials, raw materials and energy, led to temporarily high inflation rates (Morgan Stanley, 2023). After more than a decade of low and zero interest rate policy, this turnaround in interest rates increased the financing costs for existing properties and development projects. In the UK, variable interest rates tended to be the norm. The impact on Germany, where extended fixed-interest periods were more widespread, was delayed until loans expired and refinancing was required.

At the same time, yields rose again on fixed-income securities, such as time deposits, federal bonds and corporate bonds, resulting in large outflows of investor capital from the CRE sector. Particularly in the UK, CRE lenders increasingly employed back leverage to increase their capital resources. In loan-on-loan structures, loans are advanced to lenders by back leverage providers, typically traditional banks (Bank of England, 2024b; ECB, 2024b). Seemingly, banks did not favour direct exposure to the underlying assets, but imposed stricter reporting requirements on lenders than institutional investors had done. There had also been a noticeable shift of CRE debt funds into new market segments and asset classes, particularly private and public infrastructure such as data and logistics centres, solar plants, schools, and hospitals.

In view of the property market crisis, the alternative investment fund industry also gradually became a source of greater concern to financial regulators. As will be explained, the second most significant interfering factor was the status of the financial regulation of CRE debt funds. Financial regulation did not directly impact the performance of loans, but it did do so indirectly, as it constituted the regulatory framework for the loan risk management practices of debt funds. Adopted by the European Parliament and the European Council, the AIFMD regulates the managers of alternative investment funds that were not covered by the Undertakings for Collective Investment in Transferable Securities Directive (UCTIS) (alfi, 2014). The AIFMD affected both debt funds based in the EU and those from non-EU countries who wished to market their funds in the EU. In Germany, the directive was transposed into national law in the form of the German Capital Investment Code. After more than a decade since the AIFMD was first enforced, the European Parliament and European Council adopted the amending directive AIFMD II (2024), scheduled to come into force in the EU member states in 2026, two years after publication in the Official Journal of the EU. The most significant changes introduced by AIFMD II relate to debt funds, introducing not only additional credit risk restrictions but also requiring lenders to implement effective strategies, procedures and processes for granting and managing loans, and for the ongoing assessment of credit risks (GrenbergTraurig, 2023). Since the AIFMD II was only adopted in the year this thesis was submitted and would not come into force for another two years, its progressive effects on loan risk management practices could at this point in time only be the subject of speculation.

Mention should also be made of the EU's strategy on sustainable finance setting new guidelines for companies in an effort to redirect capital flows towards sustainable investments. As far as the real estate industry is concerned, the EU specified under which conditions construction, renovation and acquisition activities were considered to be aligned with the *EU taxonomy framework to facilitate sustainable investment* (European Parliament Regulation 2020/852—EU Taxonomy, 2020). In terms of the taxonomy, sustainable finance is understood as an approach that aims to (i) direct capital into sustainable economic activities; (ii) reduce environmental and social risks for investors and investees; and (iii) ensure long-term economic growth. Debt funds that can demonstrate sustainable practices increasingly have a competitive advantage, as they are more likely to secure capital from investors, who in turn are increasingly requesting reporting on key figures in line with the Sustainable Finance Disclosure Regulation (European Parliament Regulation 2019/2088—SFDR, 2019) and the Corporate Sustainability Reporting Directive (European Parliament Directive 2022/2464—CSRD, 2022). Even though the EU Taxonomy seemed to have receded somewhat into the background in the face of the wider commercial real estate crisis, it is assumed that sustainable funds, also known as responsible investment funds or green funds, will increasingly enjoy competitive advantages.

> *The problem is that everyone assumed that interest rates would remain at zero. Many business plans were based on that [...] and now interest rates have gone up and will remain high and I think there was simply a misjudgement on the part of many investors and [debt funds] that they did not expect that at all [...] And then you also have a few other issues, both in terms of how the economy as a whole will develop and the ESG, especially in office buildings. Is there even enough money to bring older buildings up to standard? In terms of the economic cycle, we are currently in a corrective phase [...] You now have problems with overvaluation, interest rates, more equity, and the investments necessary for ESG. It's all coming together.*
>
> *Industry expert, UK*

Even though sustainability was becoming increasingly relevant, it was pointed out that more legal enforcement might be needed to ensure that market participants were not just paying lip service to it. Increasing self-regulation of debt funds was nonetheless observed, as investors' sustainability-related requirements were already creating significant market competition.

The ESG issue creates constant pressure. We are currently raising money for a new fund that is very ESG-focussed. Investors need a lot of ESG in their portfolios, but they still want high returns, and that does not work. This regulation is keeping us very busy because if you want to implement everything, you have projects that no longer generate any returns.

Industry expert, Germany

While ESG reporting was already taken into account in due diligence reviews, it can be assumed that the Sustainable Finance Reporting Directive and Corporate Sustainability Reporting Directive requirements will further professionalise loan risk management from a sustainability perspective.

6.2.4 Concluding Remarks

Based on the key findings of subchapter 6.2, the concluding remarks provide a summarised response to the respective research questions. This subchapter connected the identified key characteristics of effective loan risk management, derived from practical application, with an examination of the causal mechanisms between these practices and loan performance, in the process considering wider contextual factors. Consequently, the analysis evolved from organisational structures and operational procedures, to a bird's eye view of the anchoring of debt funds in the wider CRE market. These research findings are novel, as existing peer-reviewed publications did not venture into the field of the CRE alternative lending, and academic literature was equally silent on the causal mechanisms operating between debt funds' loan risk management practices and loan performance.

The empirical findings regarding the CRE alternative lending space confirmed the causal proposition that loan risk management practices affected the performance of loans. Key factors that enabled debt funds to get ahead of the curve were identified as (i) effective control mechanisms between functional units in decision-making processes; (ii) proactive and timely mitigation of distressed situations; (iii) respectful, mutually beneficial lender-borrower relationships; (iv) qualified credit risk personnel; and (v) appropriate information technology. Even if professional practices could not always prevent loan default and the workout and restructuring of distressed loans, they did create the best possible conditions for consensual solutions.

As the most significant external influencing factor, the economic cycle had direct and indirect effects on loan performance. In the highly competitive environment of the real estate market upturn that lasted for more than a decade, debt funds seized investment opportunities to employ the capital that investors had eagerly provided. The concerns of market analysts who recognised early signs of a developing real estate bubble were largely dismissed at the time. Inevitably, the subsequent series of global crises severely impacted the CRE sector. The combination of (i) lower demand for property investments; (ii) the decline in the rental demand for certain property types, e.g. office space; (iii) an increase in expected capital expenditure; (iv) increased financing costs; (v) lower availability of debt for property investments; and (vi) an uninspiring outlook for economic growth, led to an increase in property yields. As the usage, prices and valuations of commercial property assets fell, investor capital increasingly deserted the CRE sector. Meanwhile, CRE debt funds leveraged the loan-on-loan structures that were typically offered by traditional banks as back-leverage providers. Debt funds also seized opportunities in new market segments, particularly in private and public infrastructure. More stringent demands for professional loan risk management structures and processes were increasingly expected from CRE debt funds by institutional investors, who were nervously eyeing the growing number of distressed situations. As back-leverage providers, traditional banks were also imposing stricter reporting requirements.

Even though its impact on the performance of loans was rather indirect, the second-most-significant interfering factor was the status of the supervision and regulation of debt funds. As a result of the property market crisis, the alternative investment fund industry gradually attracted more interest from financial regulators, who had kept the sector on a loose leash for more than a decade. As debt funds tightened their belts to mitigate the impact of the crisis, they also had to deal with the increasing requirements of sustainable finance in order to prevail in a competitive, ever-narrowing market.

In subchapter 6.3, the conclusions of subchapters 6.1 and 6.2, which were derived from open-ended qualitative research, are complemented by the findings of a small-scale survey among industry experts and practitioners.

6.3 Ahead of the Curve? Findings of a Small-Scale Survey

The methodological approach of using open-ended questions for semi-structured expert interviews was complemented by a small-scale survey, in which all interviewees participated. This third subchapter is divided into two sections, namely (i) purpose and approach; and (ii) analysis of the results of the small-scale survey.

6.3.1 Purpose and Approach

While the findings of this small-scale survey are not claimed to be statistically significant, they illustrate the views and perspectives of respondents on issues relevant to this thesis. The structure of the survey allowed for the allocation of response tendencies to the four key groups of respondents: (A) lenders; (B) borrowers; (C) intermediaries (i.e., loan servicers, law firms); and (D) subject matter experts (i.e., regulators, market analysts). As the data analysis will show, the further categorisation of respondents groups into sub-groups was particularly informative.

Interviewees' personal opinions on and attitudes towards pre-formulated statements were assessed on a five-point Likert scale, where low numbers indicate disagreement and high numbers, agreement. The Likert scale goes back to the American social researcher Rensis Likert (1932) and measures nuanced opinions and perceptions of respondents on predefined statements.

This Likert scale survey assessed responses to a series of eight statements:

I. CRE debt funds do not focus enough on risk management aspects in loan management.
II. CRE debt funds have the right information technology tools to manage loan-level risks.
III. Loan management functions at CRE debt funds are adequately staffed.
IV. Poor quality and/or delays of information are major sources of loan-level risks.
V. The timing of mitigation measures has a significant influence on loan performance.
VI. CRE debt funds have an effective relationship with their borrower counterparts.
VII. CRE debt funds should be more regulated.
VIII. CRE debt funds are able to manage risks more effectively than banks.

A methodological consideration was that all items were formulated as strictly positive or negative statements. The Likert scale is based on the assumption that the further respondents' attitudes deviate from those evinced in the statements, the more the statements will be rejected. The response options for an item represent the degree to which respondents agree or disagree with the statement. The possible answers were coded as natural numbers and arranged in ascending order: 1) disagree completely; 2) disagree somewhat; 3) neither disagree nor agree; 4) agree somewhat; and 5) agree completely.

The wording of the statements was randomly either positive or negative (or neutral) with respect to the expected responses to avoid certain response biases, such as confirmation or anchor bias (Kalton & Schuman, 1982; Smith & Hyman, 1950), as shown in Table 6.2.

Table 6.2 Survey questions, results and phrasing directions w.r.t. expected results

Statement	Phrased +/− vs. expected result	1	2	3	4	5
I CRE debt funds do not focus enough on the risk management aspects of loan management	+	8	14	7	21	2
II CRE debt funds have the right information technology tools to manage loan-level risks	−	9	19	17	6	1
III Loan management functions at CRE debt funds are adequately staffed	−	7	17	14	11	3
IV Poor quality and/or delays of information are major sources of loan-level risks	+	2	3	3	18	26
V The timing of mitigation measures has a significant influence on loan performance	+	0	0	2	11	39

(continued)

Table 6.2 (continued)

Statement	Phrased +/− vs. expected result	1	2	3	4	5
VI CRE debt funds have an effective relationship with their borrower counterparts	−	0	0	24	16	12
VII CRE debt funds should be more regulated	O	14	8	14	13	3
VIII CRE debt funds are able to manage risks more effectively than banks	O	6	9	9	20	8

Source: author

Responses to the individual items of Likert scales are formally ordinal or rank-scaled, so results on each statement can therefore be summarised by the median or mode as a position parameter. Statistically speaking, the use of the mean value is only permissible if it is ensured that the Likert scale is formulated symmetrically, and the scale points are actually interpreted as equally spaced by all respondents.

6.3.2 Analysis of the Small-Scale Survey Results

The total response scores for individual statements are shown in Fig. 6.8. Statement order bias could not be ruled out, but was assumed to be of lesser relevance. It was the author's impression that respondents reflected carefully on each statement, basing their responses on their own experience, and without being unduly influenced by the context of the previous statement. No extreme response bias was observed, with the tendency being rather to avoid extreme answers and opt for "somewhat" or neutral responses. The histogram of all responses by the possible response types (1) disagree completely to 5) agree completely) is shown in Fig. 6.7.

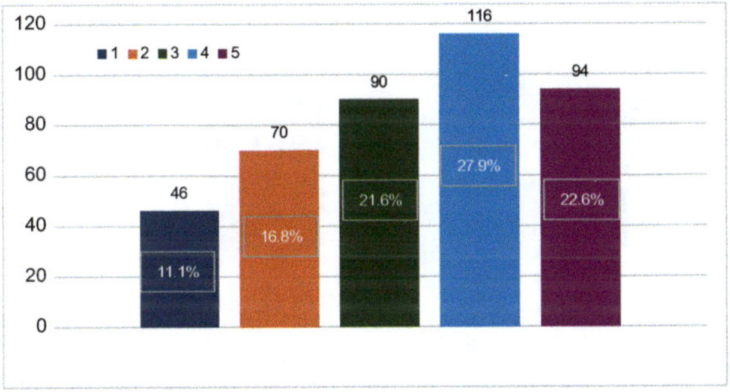

Fig. 6.7 Distributions of all survey responses by response type. (Source: o. i.)

As shown in Fig. 6.8, no conclusive findings emerged for statements I, III, VII and VIII. For statement I, respondents exhibited a tendency towards noting that there was a lack of focus on risk management. Likewise, for statement III, there was a tendency to note a lack of sufficient staffing of loan risk management units at debt funds, with a large number (14) of neutral responses from respondents who seemingly had insufficient insight into staffing levels. Statement VII on market regulation was of particular interest, as the responses were skewed towards the extremes. Here, two opposing positions were evident, one against more regulation and one in favour of more regulation. However, more respondents (14) were strongly against more regulation than were in favour of it (3). This finding seemed to reflect opinions expressed in expert interviews that one of the key advantages of debt funds was their greater flexibility resulting from their being subject to less stringent market regulation. While the findings on statement VIII were rather inconclusive, a slight tendency could be perceived towards agreement that debt funds were able to manage their credit risks more effectively than banks.

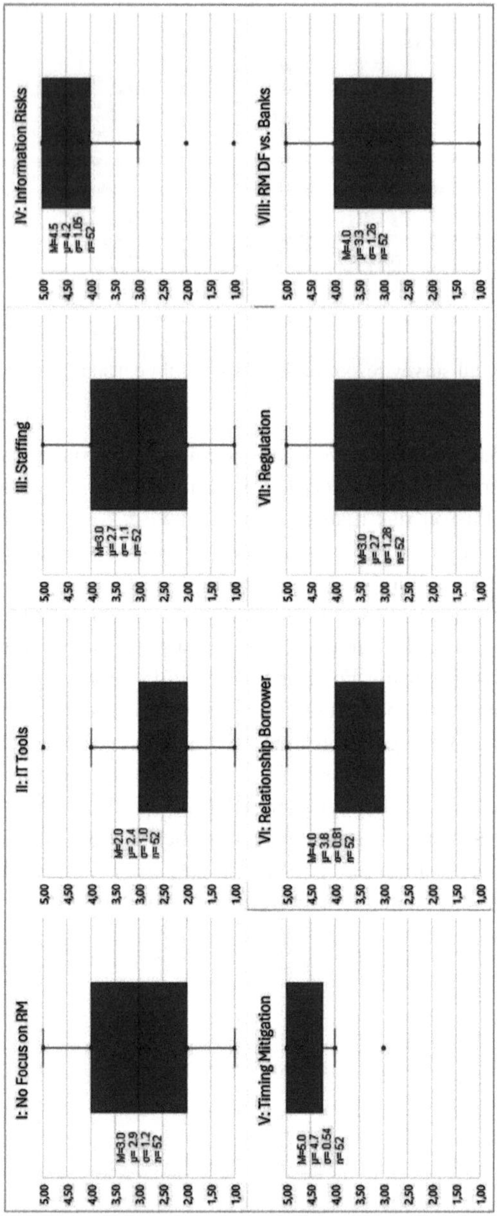

Fig. 6.8 Results of the small-scale survey (whisker charts). (Source: o. i.)

More conclusive findings were obtained for statements II, IV, V, and VI. Here, the findings also strongly confirmed the statements made in the qualitative expert interviews, which were presented in detail in Sect. 6.1. Respondents negated statement II, thereby effectively asserting that debt funds did not have sufficient information technology tools to effectively manage their loan-level risks. Agreement with statement IV on poor information quality or delays in information becoming available being driver of loan-level risks was conclusive, with a μ of 4.2 and 48 respondents agreeing with the statement. Even stronger agreement was observed for statement V on the timing of mitigation measures significantly influencing loan performance, where 50 out of the 52 respondents agreed, with 39 strongly agreeing. The positively phrased statement VI relating to the effectiveness of the relationships between lenders and borrowers was also predominantly confirmed, with a μ of 3.8 and a comparatively dense σ of 0.8. Interestingly, while 24 respondents remained neutral, no respondents negated the statement either strongly ("completely disagree") or more weakly ("somewhat disagree").

A detailed breakdown of average responses (μ) by respondent groups is shown in Fig. 6.9, which highlights agreement and disagreement with selected statements by groups of respondents, relative to the overall scores of all respondents. From a comparative perspective, insights on the views of different stakeholders involved in loan risk management were provided. The most significant deviation was observed for statement VIII, where the borrower group deviated from the overall average by −1.04 points towards disagreement. This difference was even more pronounced relative to the lenders, who generally responded more positively than the overall average of + 0.43 points. With −0.73 points, borrowers expressed more negative opinions on the adequate staffing of debt funds' loan risk management units (statement III). With −0.66 points, subject matter experts were less positive than the overall average with regard to lenders having an effective relationship with borrowers (statement VI).

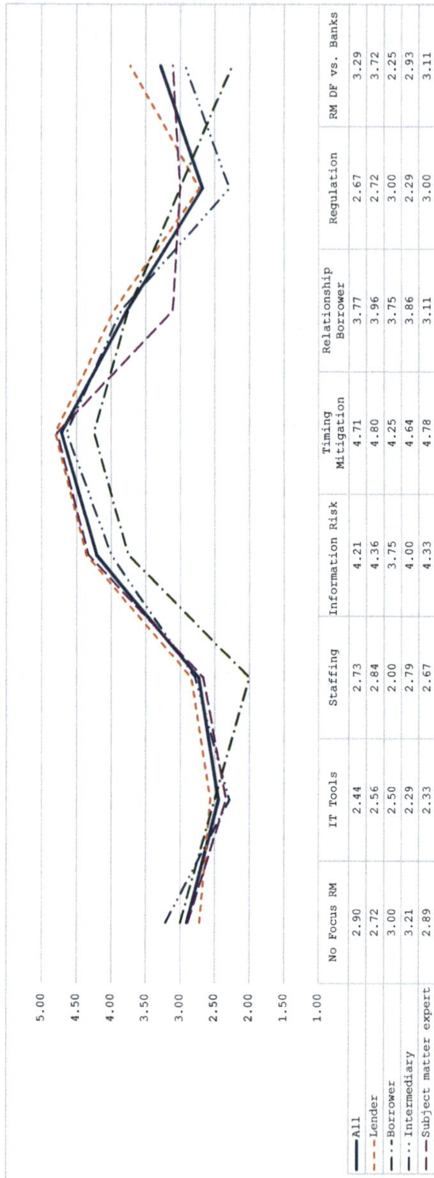

Fig. 6.9 Total scores, by groups of respondents. (Source: o. i.)

In order to refine understanding of the views of the responder groups, the subgroups lenders (A) and intermediaries (C) were further subdivided into senior debt fund managers (A.1) and loan risk managers (A.2); and loan servicers (C.1) and law firms (C.2) (Fig. 6.10). For statement I, representatives of law firms (C.2) had a more negative view (by + 0.85 points) on debt funds' focus on risk management, while senior debt fund managers (A1) not surprisingly held more positive views (−0.81 points) on the matter. The largest deviations occurred for statement II, with senior debt fund managers (A.1) and representatives of law firms (C.2) holding more positive views on available information technology tools (by 0.74 and 0.81 points, respectively), and loan managers at debt funds (A.2) and loan servicers (C.1) holding more negative views (by −0.44 points and −0.66 points, respectively). For statements III and IV, only the scoring of law firm representatives (C.2) deviated from the otherwise similar views, albeit quite strongly so, by 0.98 and 0.96 points, respectively. The reasons for these deviations could only be surmised, as external law firms usually had little insight into the personnel structures of debt funds and the reporting intervals of borrowers. No noticeable deviation was observed for statements V and VI. A lower degree of agreement for statement VII, relating to the market regulation of debt funds, was expressed by loan servicers, by −0.56 points. For statement VIII, views bifurcated: more than all other groups, debt fund senior management (A.1) viewed debt funds as being better able to manage loan-level risks than banks, by + 0.98 points. Although much less pronounced at + 0.29 points, this opinion was shared by loan risk managers (A.2). Interestingly, loan servicers (C.1) and representatives of law firms (C.2) expressed significantly different opinions, with −0.51 and −0.29 points, respectively.

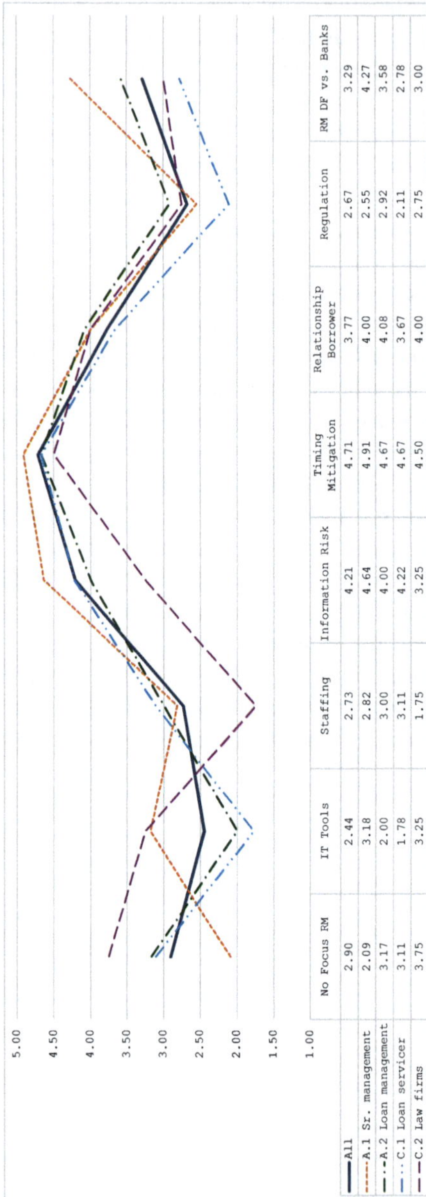

	No Focus RM	IT Tools	Staffing	Information Risk	Timing Mitigation	Relationship Borrower	Regulation	RM DF vs. Banks
All	2.90	2.44	2.73	4.21	4.71	3.77	2.67	3.29
A.1 Sr. management	2.09	3.18	2.82	4.64	4.91	4.00	2.55	4.27
A.2 Loan management	3.17	2.00	3.00	4.00	4.67	4.08	2.92	3.58
C.1 Loan servicer	3.11	1.78	3.11	4.22	4.67	3.67	2.11	2.78
C.2 Law firms	3.75	3.25	1.75	3.25	4.50	4.00	2.75	3.00

Fig. 6.10 Total scores, by selected respondent subgroups. (Source: o. i.)

In summary, the results of the small-scale survey were in line with the findings of the qualitative analysis. Opinions on the lack of adequate information technology tools and on the significance of functional relationships between lenders and borrowers strongly confirmed key aspects of the findings regarding loan risk management practices. The most significant finding was the confirmation of the interrelationship between information dissymmetry and the importance of timely and foresighted implementation of mitigation measures, and the effects this interrelationship had on loan performance. The survey findings thus significantly contributed to the confirmation of the ex-ante impact model. Of particular interest for this study were the differences between the opinions of the various respondent groups and sub-groups observed in the small-scale survey. Divergences between the opinions of hierarchical levels of lenders, i.e. strategic management, and operations, as well as between those of the internal management of debt funds and external intermediaries, were particularly evident.

6.4 Excursus: Reflections on Macroeconomic Impacts of Debt Funds' Loan Performance

As discussed, the analysis of the macroeconomic impacts of debt funds' loan performance lay beyond the scope of this research study. Due to their significance, however, reflections of interviewees on more systemic impacts of CRE debt funds' loan performance on the broader economic context should be presented and summarised as a brief excursus. This attempt to capture the three-tiered perspective from loan risk management practices, to loan performance, and to broader economic impacts, is based on perceptions, not hard data, yet should add value to the academic outcome of the thesis, even if only to a limited degree. As outlined in the synopsis of the author's literature review, peer-reviewed academic research has hitherto primarily focussed on the systemic and structural problems in the real estate sector that led to the GFC. With regard to commercial property, the focus has been on the determinants of risk tolerance in the banking sector, and the impact of regulations on reducing bank risk in commercial real estate lending. Since academic research has largely overlooked the alternative lending space in general and CRE debt funds in particular, the following reflections on the macroeconomic impacts of debt funds' loan performance break new ground.

The term "systemic risk" lies at the core of this exploration. Systemic risk is generally understood as the possibility that events at company levels could trigger severe instability or even the collapse of entire financial systems or markets (ESRB, 2019b). Preconditions leading to such severe impacts are the significance of the industries for the overall economy and their interlinkages and interdependencies. In these cases, the failure of a single entity or cluster of entities can result in a cascade of failure, which can potentially bankrupt or bring down an entire system or market (BIS, 2004; Davis & Zhu, 2011; Herring & Wachter, 1998; Levitin & Wachter, 2013; Pavlov & Wachter, 2004). In order to reduce systemic risks, the traditional banking sector became subject to strict regulatory supervision and publicity requirements (Bank for International Settlements, 2003; BCBS, 2015, 2017a, 2017b). However, the fact that banks became more risk-averse due to capital rules and the risk weighting that were introduced opened the door to what is referred to as regulatory arbitrage, where transactions are shifted out of the prudential parameter to less regulated sectors (Investment Property Forum-IPF, 2017; PGIM 2021b). As explained, CRE debt funds occupied a particular niche in the sphere of commercial real estate lending, capitalising from the gradual post-GFC retreat of banks and other traditional capital sources.

Given the recent CRE crisis, a question of interest was whether the industry experts who were surveyed were more inclined to believe that CRE debt funds had the potential to mitigate systemic risk, or that regulatory arbitrage was instead gradually developing into a matter of concern. One school of thought proved to be dominant: debt funds were more likely to mitigate systemic risks. It must be noted, however, that opinions were usually expressed tentatively, with qualifying "ifs" and "buts". The main argument put forward was that due to the diversification of lending sources and credit risks, debt funds added liquidity, flexibility and resilience to CRE capital markets. The understanding of systemic risk was primarily associated with the traditional banking business, which had reduced its CRE exposure post-GFC, thus allowing alternative sources of capital to enter the market from which they had withdrawn. While banks became cautious when it came to commercial property financing, segments of the real estate sector that required credit had no option but to seek out alternative sources of funding. By filling these market and credit gaps, CRE debt funds played an important role in supporting stability and growth in the commercial property market (CBRE, 2023).

Nevertheless, even if debt funds undeniably added value to the commercial property market, and even if they did not constitute systemic risk comparable to that of traditional banks, the market risks associated with alternative lending were not entirely dismissed. The significance of these market risks largely depended on both the overall number of debt funds affected, and the size of the companies concerned.

> *But there is a tipping point, isn't there? If enough of them [debt funds] are making fairly foolish investment decisions on the debt side, the leverage will be too high and the risk portfolio will be too large, and they have not done their diligence properly. That could start to become systemic, I guess. But I do not know. Have we tested that? I mean, hopefully interest rates have past their peak.*
>
> *Partner, law firm, UK*

By its very nature, collapses of institutional, bank-like CRE debt funds with substantial loan ticket sizes could have significant impacts on the industry. The market segment of alternative lending would undoubtedly receive more attention from regulators if its volume and market share continued to increase. In this regard, three aspects were regarded as critical: (i) the potential for market distortions caused by products and prices in the CRE sector being driven; (ii) possible capital losses of insurance companies and pension funds administering the investments of private policyholders and future pensioners; and (iii) the consequences of an increase in back-leveraged transactions, particularly in the UK property market. Although the order in which these aspects are listed provides the structure for what follows below, it should not be taken as a ranking of their severity.

Market distortions could arise, for example, if already overheated commercial property markets were to be further fuelled by speculative investments and risky transactions. Widening gaps between property values and their earning capacities could lead to property bubbles, potentially affecting wider markets. Conversely, the combination of lower demand for commercial property investments and the decline in the rental performance of these properties might cause debt funds to sell due to liquidity pressures. In turn, this could lead to devaluations at banks and holders of defaulted loans filing for bankruptcy. In Germany, however, the current market share of debt funds was not yet considered to be large enough for downward price pressure to initiate market disruptions that would pose a threat to financial stability.

Opinions were divided on the potential systemic impact of capital losses of insurance companies and pension funds. One somewhat simplistic view was that bad investments and capital losses of insurance companies and pension funds would only have negative impacts on the prosperity of private policyholders and future pensioners. Even if these risks were not comparable to cascading system failures in the event of the insolvency of traditional financial institutions, more prudent views recognised the potential for systemic risk in the event of loan defaults occurring on a wider scale. The key differences between bank failures in wider financial crises, and the impact of substantial capital losses by insurance companies and pension funds would be that the latter affected private individuals with certain time buffers, and that these private individuals might belong to specific social groups, and not the general populace.

> *This is where the circle closes. What does the regulator have to say about the current situation? To be honest, I think a kind of silent expropriation is taking place. Now that we have private debt, we no longer have to protect granny, who is a savings account holder at a credit institute, by bailing out the banks. This credit risk was shifted to the private debt sector, and that was a success. But who is acting as the capital provider now? Of course these are not the grannies with their savings books. But it may be a whole host of German pensioners who have paid into their life insurances, occupational disability insurances and other insurance products. Here, we still have the credit risk of a loan default. By the time depositors in the pension products etc. will realise that something has defaulted, it is so long that no one notices. Therefore, I think that from a national policy perspective, [the regulator] has been successful in outsourcing risks. But these risks have not gone away from an economic perspective. They still affect the same people. But everything occurs at a different time. And it perhaps affects different social groups.*
>
> *Partner, law firm, Germany*

In the UK and the US, in particular, back-leverage provided by investment banks to debt funds boosted market liquidity. Through loan-on-loan structures, debt fund lenders sought additional capital from traditional finance providers that did not want direct exposure to the underlying CRE assets. The expression "hidden leverage" implied that regulators could not identify these loans on banks' balance sheets as CRE exposures. In this way, the traditional banking sector indirectly exposed itself to higher risk profiles. The growing relevance of back leverage funding, in which traditional banks took senior tranches of loans, was attributed to positive self-regulatory effects of debt funds that had to comply with stricter supervision and more stringent reporting requirements.

> *However, it would be naïve to think that there is no impact if these debt funds overextended and lend too much. If banks would start to enforce their loan-on-loan positions and force asset sales, it will impact wider valuations and it will filter back.*
>
> *Loan manager, loan servicer, Ireland*

There was broad agreement that debt funds had a significant role to play in the commercial property market, and that their market share will continue to grow in the years to come. The market development in recent years differed considerably between the UK and the US on the one side and continental Europe on the other. Recently, non-bank lenders have been accounting for 10% to 20% of the CRE market share in continental Europe, including Germany (Empira, 2023; PGIM, 2023), but as much as 45% of new lending in the UK (Bayes Business School, 2024). The UK market was consequently considered to be already matured and more saturated, whereas Germany was considered to be more of a growth market for alternative lending. The role of the UK as a forerunner in Europe was attributed in particular to corresponding growth impulses in the US, where the market share of non-bank lenders stood at approximately 60% (PGIM, 2022, 2023). Even if the potential for growth in the European market were assumed, the pace of market expansion would depend on various factors, in particular wider economic development and its effects on the commercial property market. It was expected that before the next cyclical phase of economic growth, there would be market adjustments in which the current number of lenders in the CRE market would initially decrease due to insolvencies and takeovers. Under the increasingly watchful eyes of regulators and with the growing demands of investors (EBA, 2024, p. 115, 2024, p. 5; ECB, 2024b), the screws are set to be tightened. Overhead costs will rise further, which will make it more difficult for smaller debt funds to compete in raising and deploying capital. Therefore, it is expected that after a phase of market restructuring, involving liquidations and mergers of market participants, the consolidation of the CRE debt fund industry will set in, characterised by less fragmentation and substantial growth of fewer, but more established companies.

Conclusions 7

This final chapter summarises the novel contribution of the research study to academic debate, and by way of conclusion, responds to the empirical research questions by reducing complexity and consolidating the key findings to allow for a plausible verification of the posited causal mechanisms. The derived implications for management practice, for regulatory supervision, and for academic debates in the researched field are presented.

7.1 Summary of Findings

This study brought light to bear on a research field which has largely been neglected in peer-reviewed academic research, and was able to present novel findings that should be of equal interest to economics scholars and industry practitioners. Given that the market share of debt funds in the commercial property market was already significant, albeit in varying degrees in the UK and continental Europe, and that industry experts predicted further growth potential, the absence of wider scientific research on the subject was all the more remarkable. This study was timely given the significant impact of the recent global crises on property markets and the risks associated with regulatory arbitrage, which have gradually been developing into matters of concern. The focus of this study on the plausible effects of risk management on loan performance therefore seemed to be more pressing than ever, especially in view of the potential macroeconomic impacts emanating from the alternative lending space. This is underscored by the recent growth in interest shown by regulatory bodies, which is expected to have spillover effects on academic research in the short to medium term.

W. Hammel, *Loan Risk Management of Commercial Real Estate Debt Funds*,
https://doi.org/10.1007/978-3-658-48912-0_7

Evidence plausibly substantiated the posited causal mechanism between the effective loan risk management of CRE debt funds and loan performance. Multi-causality was recognised, but with the caveat that the most prominent contextual factors at play were macroeconomic developments and their effects on CRE markets—the very developments which debt fund risk management, as a core task, should have assessed in order for their effects, where necessary and as far as possible, to be mitigated. The effectiveness of risk management practices depended on various organisational and operational factors which were interlinked and mutually dependent, including corporate structures, processes, cultures and relationships, and not least resources and infrastructure provided to the responsible units.

Presented as predictions about the research outcomes, ex-ante propositions relating to the analytical sub-questions were tested. Data analysis allowed for the following conclusions, based on the verification of the ex-ante propositions:

- Ex-ante proposition I, that the company size of debt funds, particularly during their growth phases with limited financial and personnel resources, posed administrative and operational challenges to loan risk management, and limited portfolios provided little headroom for balancing off loan-by-loan losses, was confirmed. The fact that real estate market upswings were not particularly conducive to prioritising back-office staffing levels also applied to larger debt funds, which, however, usually had ample capital and resources to mitigate adverse impacts during economic downturns.
- Ex-ante proposition II, that as the main focus of debt funds was predominantly on profit maximisation rather than on loss minimisation, resource-intensive but non-revenue generating loan risk management units were often ignored, was confirmed. That said, a gradual change in awareness was observed in the face of the ongoing crises in CRE industries.
- Ex-ante proposition III, that due to so-called disaster myopia, defined as the cognitive dissonance of ignoring risks that seem less likely than they actually are, especially during economic upswings with rising property values, debt funds often understood risk management primarily as credit risk assessment at loan underwriting, and to a lesser degree as an ongoing management task, was partially confirmed. Corporate structures and processes were too diverse, particularly in the spectrum between more and less institutionalised companies, for this statement to be universally confirmed.
- Ex-ante proposition IV, that in relation to borrowers, lenders were exposed to an information asymmetry which needed to be overcome in order for them to embark on more timely and collaborative solutions in the event of loan default,

was confirmed. Comprehensive and timely communication between lenders and borrowers was generally welcomed, but should, however, be reciprocal. There was little evidence that information was being deliberately withheld. Nonetheless, it was pointed out that data processing by intermediaries might result in the selective accessing of information.

- Ex-ante proposition V, that the receipt of non-standardised reports (which could therefore not be meaningfully compared) from borrowers and servicers, which had to be processed by loan risk management units in time-consuming work processes, led to reduced efficiency, while personal interaction between borrowers, lenders and servicers remained restricted to the minimum, was partially confirmed. While the first dimension of the hypothesis, which relates to the lack of standardisation in borrower reporting, could be fully confirmed, there was little indication that personal interaction between lenders and borrowers was held in low regard. That being said, it was important to ensure that PLs also received appropriate attention.
- Ex-ante proposition VI, that the units responsible for loan risk management often used outdated information technologies, requiring more time for the completion of tasks and thereby leading to inefficiency in workflows, was confirmed. The exceptions of more tech-savvy debt funds included in the survey boosted the argument in favour of the application of more innovative and future-oriented systems.
- Ex-ante proposition VII, that as debt funds were not subject to strict regulatory supervision and publicity requirements, they often exposed themselves to increased levels of credit risk due to the higher allocation of riskier loans, as they tended to invest in asset classes, regions and capital structures from which traditional financial institutes had withdrawn, was partially confirmed. Although the regulatory environment impacted investment behaviour, it was not the only influencing factor. In their own interest, investors should demand appropriate checks and balances in decision-making processes. In this competitive market, however, smaller debt funds in their growth phases were particularly exposed to credit risks, as new business was vital for their economic survival.
- Ex-ante proposition VIII, that against the backdrop of the green transition, debt funds increasingly directed their lending efforts towards ESG-accredited projects, with the aim of avoiding compliance risks that might turn into loan-level risks, was partially confirmed. The impact of climate change on real estate portfolios was just one of many challenges that debt funds faced, others being elevated interest rates, high inflation, and rising construction costs.

Even so, investors had increasing bargaining power as market capital became scarcer, which also affected the enforcement of ESG criteria.

- Ex-ante proposition IX, that in contrast to the portfolio management practices of banks, the loan-by-loan risk monitoring of many debt funds exposed them to higher concentration risks, was partially confirmed. The higher exposure to concentration risks was more widespread among smaller, less institutionalised funds that focussed exclusively on specific asset classes and categories and geographic areas.
- Ex-ante proposition X, that of efficient loan risk management included the recognition of personnel resources and required qualifications; high quality loan underwriting; efficiency gains through state-of-the-art information technology; standardisation of reporting by borrowers and servicers; clear reporting and communication lines; and the timely implementation of mitigation measures for credit risks, which depended on trustworthy collaboration between the stakeholders, was confirmed.
- Ex-ante proposition XI, that even if primary effects such as an increase in maximum returns of individual loans would not materialise through effective loan risk management, the early mitigation of borrowers' payment defaults should result in the secondary effect of minimising potential losses, was confirmed. Moreover, suggestions were made as to how loan risk management units could better demonstrate performance-related returns.
- Finally, ex-ante proposition XII, that notwithstanding multicausality, there were contextual factors that could be assumed to have had particular influence on loan performance; market risks were precisely what should have been monitored, as their potential to cause credit risks should have been evaluated, and the likelihood of their being influenced by mitigation measures should have been realistically assessed, was confirmed.

Table 7.1 summarises the above-mentioned findings of this research.

Table 7.1 Summary of Results.

#	Ex-ante proposition	Confirmation level
I	The company size of debt funds, particularly during their growth phases with limited financial and personnel resources, posed administrative and operational challenges to loan risk management, and limited portfolios provided little headroom for balancing off loan-by-loan losses.	Confirmed
II	As the main focus of debt funds was predominantly on profit maximisation rather than on loss minimisation, resource-intensive but non-revenue generating loan risk management units were often ignored.	Confirmed
III	Due to so-called disaster myopia, defined as the cognitive dissonance of ignoring risks that seem less likely than they actually are, especially during economic upswings with rising property values, debt funds often understood risk management primarily as credit risk assessment at loan underwriting, and to a lesser degree as an ongoing management task.	Partially confirmed
IV	In relation to borrowers, lenders were exposed to an information asymmetry which needed to be overcome in order for them to embark on more timely and collaborative solutions in the event of loan default.	Confirmed
V	The receipt of non-standardised reports (which could therefore not be meaningfully compared) from borrowers and servicers, which had to be processed by loan risk management units in time-consuming work processes, led to reduced efficiency, while personal interaction between borrowers, lenders and servicers remained restricted to the minimum.	Partially confirmed
VI	The units responsible for loan risk management often used outdated information technologies, requiring more time for the completion of tasks and thereby leading to inefficiency in workflows.	Confirmed
VII	As debt funds were not subject to strict regulatory supervision and publicity requirements, they often exposed themselves to increased levels of credit risk due to the higher allocation of riskier loans, as they tended to invest in asset classes, regions and capital structures from which traditional financial institutes had withdrawn.	Partially confirmed
VIII	Against the backdrop of the green transition, debt funds increasingly directed their lending efforts towards ESG accredited projects, with the aim of avoiding compliance risks that might turn into loan-level credit risks.	Partially confirmed
IX	In contrast to the portfolio management practices of banks, the loan-by-loan risk monitoring of many debt funds exposed them to higher concentration risks.	Partially confirmed
X	Success factors of efficient loan risk management included the recognition of personnel resources and required qualifications; high quality loan underwriting; efficiency gains through state-of-the-art information technology; standardisation of reporting by borrowers and servicers; clear reporting and communication lines; and the timely implementation of mitigation measures for credit risks, which depended on trustworthy collaboration between the stakeholders.	Confirmed
XI	If primary effects such as an increase in maximum returns of individual loans would not materialise through effective loan risk management, the early mitigation of borrowers' payment defaults should result in the secondary effect of minimising potential losses.	Confirmed
XII	Notwithstanding multicausality, there were contextual factors that could be assumed to have had particular influence on loan performance; market risks were precisely what should have been monitored, as their potential to cause credit risks should have been evaluated, and the likelihood of their being influenced by mitigation measures should have been realistically assessed.	Confirmed

Source: author

In line with the qualitative research results, the findings of the small-scale survey confirmed the ex-ante impact model, in particular with regard to the interrelationships between information dissymmetry and timely and foresighted implementation of mitigation measures, and the effects they plausibly had on loan performance.

The reflections on macroeconomic impacts of debt funds' loan performance demonstrated broad consensus with the role of credit funds in mitigating systemic risks by providing liquidity, flexibility and market stability through the diversification of credit sources and credit risks. As argued, however, market risks associated with regulatory arbitrage in the alternative lending space had not escaped the vigilant market observer. Not only are the market shares of non-bank lenders expected to grow, but it is also expected that market consolidations will follow market adjustments. These market adjustments are thought to be caused by more stringent regulatory requirements and the effects of the wider economic development on commercial property markets.

7.2 Implications of this Research

The findings of this research study are relevant for academic researchers, practitioners, lawmakers and financial regulators alike.

Despite the expanding role of non-bank financial institutions, the CRE alternative lending space has remained virtually untouched by academic research. As demonstrated by the findings of this study, this rather opaque sector is not only an interesting one in itself, but also one in urgent need of the more profound understanding that can be provided by academic research. Given the increasing relevance of compliance risks emanating from the regulations for sustainable finance under the new EU taxonomy, it is expected that academic interest in the alternative lending space will increase in the near future. It can be assumed that publicity requirements for CRE debt funds will be tightened, which would allow economics scholars to access hard data, and to conduct robust and statistically relevant analyses based on loan-by-loan asset information.

This study proposed a novel research area in the field of CRE loan risk management, and it is intended to serve as an academic reference point and stimulus for economics scholars to conduct further research. The following proposals are made for areas of research interest: (i) the potential of AI-supported data management at CRE debt funds to improve data quality, reduce administrative workloads, and optimise decision-making processes based on market trend analyses; (ii) alternative lending in the real estate markets in Italy, Spain and France, in view of the specific property law frameworks pertaining in those countries, and in particular with regard to the recently adopted banking and capital markets legislation in Italy and Spain; (iii) impetus and lessons from the so-called cradle of alternative lending, the US, where the market share of non-bank lenders is even more significant, the legal system is comparatively less fragmented, and industry standards are more harmonised; and (iv) the particularly timely market adjustment, restructuring and consolidation processes in the alternative lending space in Europe, which will presumably take place before the next cyclical phase of economic growth.

Creating new knowledge and literature through academic research cannot be viewed in isolation from scientific and practice-oriented teaching through the study programmes of universities and further educational institutions. As research on alternative lending in general, and loan risk management in particular, is currently a novel academic undertaking, it is widely absent not only in university teaching and at business schools, but also in part-time programmes and educational opportunities in the real estate industry. In view of the growing market share of alternative lending, on the one hand, and the recent increase of problematic exposures, on the other, there is a significant shortage of educational opportunities for talented young people aspiring to build careers in risk management, and for loan managers with an interest in further training. For this reason, practice-oriented teaching, to which industry experts could certainly add value, is deemed to be of particular relevance. It is suggested that an interdisciplinary curriculum should include the following thematic fields: (i) real estate economics; (ii) financial modelling and data analytics; and (iii) the legal, tax and compliance aspects of real estate transactions and investments.

For practitioners, the presented key success factors for effective loan risk management, derived from and providing for practical application, should offer inspiration and guidance. These best practice guidelines provide frameworks for alternative lenders to embark on new courses for loan risk mitigation that hitherto have not been sufficiently mapped out by financial regulation and universal industry standards.

Regulatory authorities are increasingly focussing their attention on the compliance of alternative lenders with requirements of the green transition, in particular with respect to transformation to more climate-friendly buildings and sustainable construction. That being said, these research findings are also particularly timely in view of the publication of the detailed compromise text for the AIFMD II, enacted into European law in 2024 after several years of negotiation. The realisation seems to be gaining ground that effective loan risk management practices are not only essential for process optimisation, loss minimisation and competitive advantages, but are also increasingly subject to more demanding regulatory provisions. Given the current dynamics of CRE markets, comprehensive and proactive loan risk management has never been more important for safeguarding investment portfolios and getting ahead of the curve, to thrive amidst change.

References

Akerlof, G. A. (1970). The market for "lemons": Quality uncertainty and the market mechanism. *Quarterly Journal of Economics, 84*(3), 488–500.

Akin, O., Marýn, J. M., & Peydró, J.-L. (2020). Anticipating the financial crisis: Evidence from insider trading in banks. *Economic Policy, 35*(102), 213–267. https://doi.org/10.1093/epolic/eiaa012

An, X., & Pivo, G. (2020). Green buildings in commercial mortgage-backed securities: The effects of LEED and energy star certification on default risk and loan terms. *Real Estate Economics, 48*(1), 7–42. https://doi.org/10.1111/1540-6229.12228

Aria, M., & Cuccurullo, C. (2017). bibliometrix: An R-tool for comprehensive science mapping analysis. *Journal of Informetrics, 11*(4), 959–975. https://doi.org/10.1016/j.joi.2017.08.007

Association of Luxembourg Fund Industry. (2014). *Risk management under the Alternative Investment Fund Managers Directive ("AIFMD").*

BaFin. (2023). *Mindestanforderungen an das Risikomanagement - MaRisk: Rundschreiben 05/2023 (BA).* https://www.bafin.de/SharedDocs/Veroeffentlichungen/DE/Rundschreiben/2023/rs_05_2023_MaRisk_BA.html

Bank for International Settlements (2003). *Towards a macroprudential framework for financial supervision and regulation?* (BIS Working Papers No. 128). Bank for International Settlements. https://www.bis.org/publ/work128.pdf

Bank for International Settlements (2004). *Bank lending and commercial property cycles: Some cross-country evidence* (BIS Working Papers No. 150). https://www.bis.org/publ/work150.pdf

Bank for International Settlements (2023). *Building an integrated surveillance framework for highly leveraged NBFIs – lessons from the HKMA* (BIS Papers No. 137). Bank for International Settlement. https://www.bis.org/publ/bppdf/bispap137.pdf

Bank of America. (2024). *Which European CRE loans defaulted and why? March 2024 Update.*

Bank of England. (2013). *Commercial property and financial stability* (Quarterly Bulletin 2013 Q1). https://www.bankofengland.co.uk/-/media/boe/files/quarterly-bulletin/2013/commercial-property-and-financial-stability.pdf

Bank of England. (2024a). *Not-so-private questions – Speech by Nathanaël Benjamin.* https://www.bankofengland.co.uk/-/media/boe/files/speech/2024/april/speech-by-nathanael-benjamin-at-bloomberg.pdf

W. Hammel, *Loan Risk Management of Commercial Real Estate Debt Funds*,
https://doi.org/10.1007/978-3-658-48912-0

Bank of England (Ed.). (2024b). *Thematic review of private equity related financing activities: Letter to risk officers.* https://www.bankofengland.co.uk/-/media/boe/files/prudential-regulation/letter/2024/thematic-review-of-private-equity-related-financing-activities.pdf

Basel Committee on Banking Supervision. (2000). *Principles for the management of credit risk.* Bank for International Settlements. https://www.bis.org/bcbs/publ/d591.pdf

Basel Committee on Banking Supervision. (2015). *Guidance on credit risk and accounting for expected credit losses.* Bank for International Settlements. https://www.bis.org/bcbs/publ/d350.pdf

Basel Committee on Banking Supervision. (2017a). *Basel III: Finalising post-crisis reforms.* Bank for International Settlements. https://www.bis.org/bcbs/publ/d424.pdf

Basel Committee on Banking Supervision. (2017b). *High-level summary of Basel III reforms.* Bank for International Settlements. https://www.bis.org/bcbs/publ/d424_hlsummary.pdf

Basel Committee on Banking Supervision (Ed.). (2019). *CRE30: IRB approach: Overview and asset class definitions.* Bank for International Settlements.

Basel Committee on Banking Supervision. (2021a). *Principles for operational resilience.* Bank for Inernational Settlements. https://www.bis.org/bcbs/publ/d516.pdf

Basel Committee on Banking Supervision. (2021b). *Revisions to the principles for the sound management of operational risk.* Bank for International Settlements. https://www.bis.org/bcbs/publ/d515.pdf

Baselga-Pascual, L., Trujillo-Ponce, A., & Cardone-Riportella, C. (2015). Factors influencing bank risk in Europe: Evidence from the financial crisis. *North American Journal of Economics and Finance, 34*, 138–166. https://doi.org/10.1016/j.najef.2015.08.004

Bassett, W. F., & Marsh, W. B. (2017). Assessing targeted macroprudential financial regulation: The case of the 2006 commercial real estate guidance for banks. *Journal of Financial Stability, 30*, 209–228. https://doi.org/10.1016/j.jfs.2016.06.001

Bayes Business School. (2023). *European CRE lending report 2022.* University of London. https://www.bayes.citystgeorges.ac.uk/__data/assets/pdf_file/0005/725585/European-CRE-Lending-Report-YE2022.pdf

Bayes Business School. (2024). *UK CRE lending market H1 2024.*

Ben Jabra, W., Mighri, Z., & Mansouri, F. (2017). Determinants of European bank risk during financial crisis. *Cogent Economics and Finance, 5*(1), 1–20. https://doi.org/10.1080/23322039.2017.1298420

Bloom, N., & Van Reenen, J. (2007). Measuring and explaining management practices across firms and countries. *The Quarterly Journal of Economics, 122*(4), 1351–1408. https://doi.org/10.1162/qjec.2007.122.4.1351

BNP Paribas Real Estate. (2023). *Europe CRE 360: Economic outlook - Real estate perspectives.* https://www.realestate.bnpparibas.co.uk/sites/default/files/2023-09/europe-cre-360-bnppre-global-research-07092023.pdf

Brown, R. J. (2005). *Private real estate investment: Data analysis and decision making* (Academic Press advanced finance series). Elsevier Academic Press.

Brueggeman, W. B., & Fisher, J. D. (2019). *Real estate finance and investments* (16th ed., International student ed.). McGraw-Hill Education.

Bryant, W. R. (1962). *Mortgage lending: Fundamentals and practices* (2nd ed.). McGraw-Hill.

Caputo, A., & Kargina, M. (2022). A user-friendly method to merge Scopus and Web of Science data during bibliometric analysis. *Journal of Marketing Analytics*, *10*(1), 82–88. https://doi.org/10.1057/s41270-021-00142-7

Caputo, A., Pizzi, S., Pellegrini, M. M., & Dabić, M. (2021). Digitalization and business models: Where are we going? A science map of the field. *Journal of Business Research*, *123*, 489–501. https://doi.org/10.1016/j.jbusres.2020.09.053

CBRE. (2023). *The debt funding gap for European real estate*. https://mktgdocs.cbre.com/2299/a551a2ee-3973-4bf7-a935-e009385c8486-2121941228.pdf

Charmaz, K. (2014). *Constructing grounded theory* (2nd ed.). *Introducing qualitative methods*. Sage. http://www.sxf.uevora.pt/wp-content/uploads/2013/03/Charmaz_2006.pdf

Corbin, J., & Strauss, A. L. (1990). Grounded theory research: Procedures, canons and evaluative criteria. *Qualitative Sociology*, *13*(1), 3–21. https://doi.org/10.1515/zfsoz-1990-0602

Corbin, J. M., & Strauss, A. L. (2015). *Basics of qualitative research: Techniques and procedures for developing grounded theory* (4th ed.). Sage.

Dasso, J. J., & Kuhn, G. (1983). *Real estate finance* (Prentice-Hall series in real estate). Prentice-Hall.

Davis, E. P., & Zhu, H. (2011). Bank lending and commercial property cycles: Some cross-country evidence. *Journal of International Money and Finance*, *30*(1), 1–21. https://doi.org/10.1016/j.jimonfin.2010.06.005

Deakin, S., Mollica, V., & Sarkar, P. (2017). Varieties of creditor protection: Insolvency law reform and credit expansion in developed market economies. *Socio-Economic Review*, *15*(2), 359–384. https://doi.org/10.1093/ser/mww005

Demyanyk, Y., & Hasan, I. (2010). Financial crises and bank failures: A review of prediction methods. *Omega*, *38*(5), 315–324. https://doi.org/10.1016/j.omega.2009.09.007

DeNederlandscheBank(2019). *Credit risk in commercial real estate bank loans: The role of idiosyncratic versus macro-economic factors* (DNB Working Paper No. 653). https://www.dnb.nl/media/bohospy0/working-paper-no-653_tcm47-385395.pdf

Dick, M. (2010). *Der Verkauf von Non Performing Loans: Eine Analyse von NPL-Transaktionen aus Bankensicht*. (1. Auflage) [Dissertation, Universität Linz, 2009]. Gabler Research.

Echchakoui, S. (2020). Why and how to merge Scopus and Web of Science during bibliometric analysis: The case of sales force literature from 1912 to 2019. *Journal of Marketing Analytics*, *8*(3), 165–184. https://doi.org/10.1057/s41270-020-00081-9

Empira. (2023). *Real Estate Debt: Finanzierungsoptionen im Umfeld steigender Zinsen und begrenzter Bankfinanzierungen*. https://empira-invest.com/_Resources/Persistent/2/8/5/6/285652d0546097572486031ca290ad93c0317f9e/2023-Q1_Empira_Research_DE.pdf

European Banking Authority. (2017a). *Guidelines on credit institutions' credit risk management practices and accounting for expected credit losses*.

European Banking Authority. (2017b). *Guidelines on PD estimation, LGD estimation and the treatment of defaulted exposures*.

European Banking Authority. (2018). *Final guidelines on management of non-performing and forborne exposures*.

European Banking Authority. (2020). *Final report: Guidelines on loan origination and monitoring*.

European Banking Authority. (2021). *Guidelines on sound remuneration policies under Directive 2013/36/EU.*

European Banking Authority. (2024). *Risk assessment report of the European Banking Authority: July 2024.*

European Central Bank. (2017). *Guidance to banks on non-performing loans.*

European Central Bank. (2018). *Addendum to the ECB guidance to banks on non-performing loans: Supervisory expectations for prudential provisioning of non-performing exposures.*

European Central Bank. (2020). *Trends and risks in credit underwriting standards of significant institutions in the Single Supervisory Mechanism: Main findings from the credit underwriting data collection 2019.*

European Central Bank. (2022). *Commercial real estate: Connecting the dots* (Supervision Newsletter 17 August 2022).

European Central Bank. (2024a). *Commercial real estate valuations: Insights from on-site inspections* (Supervision Newsletter 14 August 2024).

European Central Bank. (2024b). *Supervising counterparty credit risk – a European perspective* [Keynote Speech]. Industry Outreach Conference on Counterparty Credit Risk Management, New York.

European Central Bank. (2024c). *Written overview ahead of the exchange of views of the Chair of the Supervisory Board of the ECB with the Eurogroup on 13 May 2024.* https://www.bankingsupervision.europa.eu/ecb/pub/pdf/ssm.written_overview240513~073c63cbf9.en.pdf

European Commission. (2013). *Commission Delegated Regulation (EU) No 231/2013 of 19 December 2012 supplementing Directive 2011/61/EU of the European Parliament and of the Council with regard to exemptions, general operating conditions, depositaries, leverage, transparency and supervision.* Office Journal of the European Union, L 83, 1-53

European Parliament & Council of the European Union. (2009). *Directive 2009/138/EC on the taking up and pursuit of the business of insurance and reinsurance (Solvency II),* Official Journal of the European Union, L 335, 1-555.

European Parliament & Council of the European Union. (2011). *Directive 2011/61/EU on alternative investment fund managers and amending directives 2003/41/EC and 2009/65/EC and regulations (EC) No 1060/2009 and (EU) No 1095/2010,* Official Journal of the European Union, L 174, 1-73.

European Parliament & Council of the European Union (2013). *Directive 2013/36/EU on access to the activity of credit institutions and the prudential supervision of credit institutions and investment firms, amending Directive 2002/87/EC and repealing Directives 2006/48/EC and 2006/49/EC,* Official Journal of the European Union, L 176, 338-436.

European Parliament & Council of the European Union. (2013). *Regulation (EU) No 575/2013 on prudential requirements for credit institutions and investment firms and amending Regulation (EU) No 648/2012*, Official Journal of the European Union, L 176, 1-337.

European Parliament & Council of the European Union. (2019). *Regulation (EU) 2019/2088 of 27 November 2019 on sustainability-related disclosures in the financial services secto*r, Official Journal of the European Union, L 317, 1-31.

European Parliament & Council of the European Union. (2020). *Regulation (EU) 2020/852 of 18 June 2020 on the establishment of a framework to facilitate sustainable investment, and amending Regulation (EU) 2019/2088,* Official Journal of the European Union, L 198, 13-43.

European Parliament & Council of the European Union. (2021). *Directive (EU) 2021/2167 on credit servicers and credit purchasers and amending Directives 2008/48/ec and 2014/17/EU*, Official Journal of the European Union, L 441, 1-46.

European Parliament & Council of the European Union. (2022). *Directive (EU) 2022/2464 of 14 December 2022 amending Regulation (EU) No 537/2014, Directive 2004/109/EC, Directive 2006/43/EC and Directive 2013/34/EU, as regards corporate sustainability reporting*, Official Journal of the European Union, L 332, 1-20.

European Parliament & Council of the European Union. (2024). *Directive (EU) 2024/927 of 13 March 2024 amending Directives 2011/61/EU and 2009/65/EC as regards delegation arrangements, liquidity risk management, supervisory reporting, the provision of depositary and custody services and loan origination by alternative investment funds*. Official Journal of the European Union, L 2024/927, 2–47.

European Public Real Estate Association. (2021). *Global real estate total markets table.*

European Public Real Estate Association/INREV. (2020). *Real estate in the real economy: Supporting growth, jobs and sustainability.* https://www.epra.com/application/files/5516/0614/4902/EPRA-INREV-Real-Estate-Real-Economy-2020-Report.pdf

European Public Real Estate Association/INREV. (2022). *Real estate in the real economy: Supporting growth, jobs and sustainability.* https://www.epra.com/application/files/9516/6861/1334/EPRA-INREV-Real_Estate_Real_FINAL_Economy_2022_Report.pdf

European Securities and Markets Authority. (2023). *Alternative investment funds (AIFs) exposures to commercial real estate.* https://www.esma.europa.eu/sites/default/files/2024-04/ESMA50-1605533872-8484_Alternative_Investment_Funds_exposures_to_commercial_real_estate 2022.pdf

European Systemic Risk Board. (2015). *Report on commercial real estate and financial stability in the EU.* https://www.esrb.europa.eu/pub/pdf/other/2015-12-28_ESRB_report_on_commercial_real_estate_and_financial_stability.pdf

European Systemic Risk Board. (2018). *Report on vulnerabilities in the EU commercial real estate sector.* https://www.esrb.europa.eu/pub/pdf/reports/esrb.report181126_vulnerabilities_EU_commercial_real_estate_sector.en.pdf

European Systemic Risk Board. (2019a). *Methodologies for the assessment of real estate vulnerabilities and macroprudential policies: Commercial real estate.* https://www.esrb.europa.eu/pub/pdf/reports/esrb.report191217_methodologies_assessment_real_estate_vulnerabilities_macroprudential_policies~15ff09ae41.en.pdf

European Systemic Risk Board. (2019b). *Recommendation of the European systemic Risk Board of 21 March 2019 amending Recommendation ESRB/2016/14 on closing real estate data gaps.*

European Systemic Risk Board. (2023). *Vulnerabilities in the EEA commercial real estate sector.* https://www.esrb.europa.eu/pub/pdf/reports/esrb.report.vulnerabilitiesEEAcommercialrealestatesector202301~e028a13cd9.en.pdf

European Systemic Risk Board. (2024). *NBFI monitor: EU non-bank financial intermediation risk monitor 2024* (9). https://www.esrb.europa.eu/pub/pdf/reports/nbfi_monitor/esrb.nbfi202406~2e211b2f80.en.pdf

Eurostat. (2017). *Commercial property price indicators: Sources, methods and issues* (2017 edition). *Statistical reports / Eurostat*. Publications Office of the European Union. https://doi.org/10.2785/050176

Federal Reserve Board. (2021). *Interagency guidelines for real estate lending policies.* Appendix C to Part 208. Federal Reserve Board –Division of Banking Supervision & Regulation.

Federal Reserve Board, Office of the Comptroller of the Currency, & Federal Deposit Insurance Corporation. (2006). *Concentrations in commercial real estate lending, Sound Risk Management Practices.* SR 07–1.

Federal Reserve Board, Office of the Comptroller of the Currency, & Federal Deposit Insurance Corporation. (2012). *Statement on prudent risk management for commercial real estate lending.* Federal Reserve Board –Division of Banking Supervision & Regulation. https://www.federalreserve.gov/boarddocs/srletters/2007/SR0701a2.pdf

Financial Conduct Authority. (2024). *Alternative investment fund manager (AIFM) hosting.*

Friese, S. (2019). *Qualitative data analysis with ATLAS.Ti* (3rd ed.). Sage.

Geltner, D. (2007). *Commercial real estate: Analysis & investments* (2nd ed.). Thomson South Western.

Gläser, J., & Laudel, G. (2010). *Experteninterviews und qualitative Inhaltsanalyse als Instrumente rekonstruierender Untersuchungen* (4. Auflage). *Lehrbuch.* VS Verlag.

Goddard, G. J., & Marcum, B. (2012). *Real estate investment: A value-based approach.* Springer. https://doi.org/10.1007/978-3-642-23527-6

Greenspan, A. (2004, October 5). *Banking: Remarks by Chairman Alan Greenspan.* American Bankers Association Annual Convention, New York. https://www.federalreserve.gov/boarddocs/speeches/2004/20041005/default.htm

GrenbergTraurig. (2023). *AIFMD II: New Regulation of Debt Funds and Other Key Changes.* https://www.gtlaw.com/en/insights/2023/12/aifmd-ii-new-regulation-of-debt-funds-and-other-key-changes

Grovenstein, R. A., Harding, J. P., Sirmans, C. F., Thebpanya, S., & Turnbull, G. K. (2005). Commercial mortgage underwriting: How well do lenders manage the risks? *Journal of Housing Economics, 14*(4), 355–383. https://doi.org/10.1016/j.jhe.2005.09.003

Gumpp, W. (2021). *Gewerbliche Immobilienfinanzierung.* C.H. Beck.

Hammel, W. (2022). *Management of loans and risks by secured credit lenders* [Literature Review]. SDA Bocconi.

Hammel, W. (2023). *Ahead of the curve: Plausible effects of loan risk management practices of CRE debt funds on loan performance* [Research Proposal]. SDA Bocconi.

Harding, J. P., & Sirmans, C. F. (2002). Renegotiation of troubled debt: The choice between discounted payoff and maturity extension. *Real Estate Economics, 30*(3), 475–503. *https://www.greeradvisors.com/research_files/choice_between_dpo_and_extension.pdf*

Herring, R. J., & Wachter, S. M. (1998). *Real estate booms and banking busts: An international perspective* [Working Paper Series, Wharton]. papers.ssrn.com.

Hinkel, R. (2024). *Alternative Finanzierung für gewerbliche Immobilien durch „Debt Fonds" und Versicherungen* [Bachelor Thesis]. Hochschule Darmstadt, Darmstadt.

INREV. (2022). *Debt vehicles universe 2022.*

INREV. (2023a). *Debt vehicles universe 2023.*

INREV. (2023b). *Navigating the changing landscape of European real estate debt.*

INREV. (2024). *Debt vehicles universe 2024.*

International Monetary Fund. (2019). *The dynamics of non-performing loans during banking crises: A new database* (IMF Working Paper 2019/272). https://doi.org/10.5089/9781513521152.001

International Monetary Fund. (2024). *Financial stability risks from commercial real estate: Germany* (Selected Issues Paper 2024/035).

Investment Property Forum. (2014). *A vision for real estate finance in the UK: Recommendations for reducing the risk of damage to the financial system from the next commercial real estate market crash.*

Investment Property Forum. (2017). *Changing sources of real estate debt capital: Facts and implications.*

Isaac, D. (2020). *Property finance* (3rd ed.). Macmillan Education UK. https://ebookcentral.proquest.com/lib/kxp/detail.action?docID=6234882

Kahneman, D. (2015). *Schnelles Denken, langsames Denken* (T. Schmidt, Trans.) (19. Auflage, Pantheon-Ausgabe). Pantheon.

Kalton, G., & Schuman, H. (1982). The effect of the question on survey responses: A review. *Journal of the Royal Statistical Society Series A: Statistics in Society*, *145*(1), 42–73.

Köchling, M., & Schalast, C. (Eds.). (2017). *Grundlagen des NPL-Geschäftes* (2., vollständig überarbeitete Auflage). Frankfurt School Verlag.

KPMG. (2022). *Private debt fund survey 2022: Harnessing the momentum of a buoyant market.* https://assets.kpmg.com/content/dam/kpmg/lu/pdf/2022_Private_Debt_Fund_Survey_secured_v02.pdf

Kromrey, H. (2002). *Empirische Sozialforschung: Modelle und Methoden der standardisierten Datenerhebung und Datenauswertung* (10., vollständig überarbeitete Auflage). VS Verlag für Sozialwissenschaften. https://doi.org/10.1007/978-3-322-93463-5

Lauer, J. (Ed.). (2021). *Praktikerhandbuch gewerbliche immobilienfinanzierung* (4. Auflage). Finanz Colloquium Heidelberg.

Leavitt, H. J. (1965). *Applied organizational change in industry: Structural, technological and humanistic approaches.* In J. G. March (Ed.), *Handbook of Organizations* (Routledge Library Editions: Vol. 20, 1st ed., pp. 1144–1170). Routledge.

Levitin, A. J., & Wachter, S. M. (2013). *The commercial real estate bubble.* Harvard Business Law Review, 3, 83–127.Harv. Bus. L. Rev., 3, 83.

Likert, R. (1932). A technique for the measurement of attitudes. *Archives of Psychology*, *22*(140), 5–55.

London Market Association. (2024, June 20). *Documents & guidelines.* https://www.lma.eu.com/documents-guidelines/documents

Loyens & Loeff. (2022). *Debt funds, Luxembourg SPVs, and the regulation of lending activities.* https://www.loyensloeff.com/insights/news--events/news/debt-funds-luxembourg-spvs-and-the-regulation-of-lending-activities/

Manz, F. (2019a). Determinants of non-performing loans: What do we know? A systematic review and avenues for future research. *Management Review Quarterly*, *69*(4), 351–389. https://doi.org/10.1007/s11301-019-00156-7

Manz, F. (2019b). *Non-performing loans: Determinants – default – divestiture.* (1st Ed.). *Nomos Universitätsschriften Betriebswirtschaftslehre: Vol. 7* [150 Seiten]. Nomos. https://doi.org/10.5771/9783748905929

Mathew, P., Issler, P., & Wallace, N. (2021). Should commercial mortgage lenders care about energy efficiency? Lessons from a pilot study. *Energy Policy*, *150.* https://doi.org/10.1016/j.enpol.2021.112137

McKinsey (Ed.). (2009). *Commercial real estate lending: Finding economic profit in a difficult industry* (McKinsey on Corporate & Investment Banking No. 9).

Merriam, S. B., & Tisdell, E. J. (2016). *Qualitative research: A guide to design and implementation* (4th ed.). Jossey-Bass.

Modina, M., & Pietrovito, F. (2014). A default prediction model for Italian SMEs: The relevance of the capital structure. *Applied Financial Economics, 24*(23), 1537–1554. https://doi.org/10.1080/09603107.2014.927566

Morgan Stanley. (2023). *The state of the CRE cycle: 10th edition – Credit conditions tighten.*

Morri, G., & Mazza, A. (Eds.). (2015). *Property finance: An international approach, with an outline of the most relevant legal issues in selected jurisdictions.* (Wiley Finance Series). Wiley. https://doi.org/10.1002/9781118764312.ch13

Mortgage Bankers Association of America. (2002). *Principles of commercial real estate: Finance.* Mortgage Bankers Association of America; Dearborn Real Estate Education.

Office of the Comptroller of the Currency. (2022). *Commercial real estate lending.*

Ono, A., Uchida, H., Udell, G. F., & Uesugi, I. (2021). Lending pro-cyclicality and macro-prudential policy: Evidence from Japanese LTV ratios. *Journal of Financial Stability, 53,* 100819. https://doi.org/10.1016/j.jfs.2020.100819

Pagourtzi, E., Assimakopoulos, V., Hatzichristos, T., & French, N. (2003). Real estate appraisal: A review of valuation methods. *Journal of Property Investment & Finance, 21*(4), 383–401. https://doi.org/10.1108/14635780310483656

Pavlov, A., & Wachter, S. M. (2004). *Real estate crashes and bank lending.* Zell/Lurie Real Estate Center.

Peridis, P. (2022). *Alternative lending: Risks, supervision, and resolution of debt funds.* Springer International Publishing; Imprint Palgrave Macmillan. https://doi.org/10.1007/978-3-031-13471-5

PGIM. (2021a). *European real estate debt: Lessons of time -A lens for the future of Europe's real estate lending landscape.*

PGIM. (2022). *Global CRE debt markets: Where are the opportunities?*

PGIM. (2023). *The long-term funding gap in European real estate.*

PGIM. (2021b). *European real estate debt: Where next? Significant opportunity for nonbank lenders to grow market share.*

Philipps, B. M. (2021). Commercial real estate loans – Categorization of an investment segment. *European Journal of Business Science and Technology, 7*(1), 5–26. https://doi.org/10.11118/ejobsat.2021.001

Private Equity Real Estate. (2023). *The real estate debt 50 2023.* https://www.perenews.com/the-real-estate-debt-50-2023/

Property Industry Alliance Debt Group. (2017). *Long-term value methodologies and real estate lending.* https://hubble-live-assets.s3.eu-west-1.amazonaws.com/crefc/file_asset/file/289/Vision_R4_long_term_value_methodologies_report__June_2017_.pdf

Property Industry Alliance Debt Group. (2018). *The CRE lending black hole: Steady gains followed by extreme pains.* https://propertyindustryalliance.org/wp-content/uploads/2018/10/cre-lending-report-final.pdf

Prymostka, L. O., & Prymostka, O. O. (2019). Risk-oriented management in the bank. *Financial and Credit Activity Problems of Theory and Practice,* 2(29), 66–72.

Real Estate Capital Europe. (2023). *Alternative lenders: The debt fund 30.*

Real Estate Capital Europe. (2024). *REC Awards 2024* (Real Estate Capital Europe No. 117).

Reinhart, C. M., & Rogoff, K. S. (2009). *This time is different: Eight centuries of financial folly.* Princeton University Press. https://doi.org/10.1515/9781400831722

Riddiough, T. J., & Wyatt, S. B. (1994). Wimp or tough guy: Sequential default risk and signaling with mortgages. *Journal of Real Estate Finance and Economics, 9*, 299–321.

Robert Morris Associates. (1984). *A special collection from the Journal of Commercial Bank Lending. Loan Review*. Robert Morris Associates.

Rottke, N. B., & Gentgen, J. (2008). Workout management of non-performing loans: A formal model on transaction cost economics. *Journal of Property Investment & Finance, 26*(1), 59–79. https://doi.org/10.1108/14635780810845163

Saft, S. M. (1991). *Commercial real estate workouts. Shepard's real estate series*. Shepard's McGraw-Hill; McGraw-Hill Information Services Co.

Scardovi, C., & Bezzecchi, A. (2019). *Banking, lending and real estate. Banking, money and international finance*. Routledge.

Shanker, H. M. (1994). A lenders guide to environmental-policy development. *Banking Law Journal, 111*(6), 540–556.

Smith, H. L., & Hyman, H. (1950). The biasing effect of interviewer expectations on survey results. *The Public Opinion Quarterly, 14*(3), 491–506. http://www.jstor.org/stable/2746005

Stokes, J., & Cox, A. (2022). Commercial real estate finance and the lending cap rate. *Journal of Property Investment and Finance 4*(1), 2-10. https://doi.org/10.1108/JPIF-10-2021-0081

The Economist (2022, July 28). How high property prices can damage the economy: A fresh strand of research studies the consequences, both in China and the rich world. *The Economist*.

Trübestein, M., & Pruegel, M. (2013). *Immobilienfinanzierung: Abkürzungen und Klassifikationen*. (Kompakt Edition). Springer Fachmedien Wiesbaden. https://doi.org/10.1007/978-3-658-00774-4

Uzzi, B., & Gillespie, J. J. (2002). Knowledge spillover in corporate financing networks: Embeddedness and the firm's debt performance. *Strategic Management Journal, 23*(7), 595–618. https://doi.org/10.1002/smj.241

van Eck, N. J., & Waltman, L. (2011). *Text mining and visualization using VOSviewer.*

VDP Die Deutschen Pfandbriefbanken. (n.d.). *Publikationen*. https://www.pfandbrief.de/site/de/vdp/publikationen/publikationen.html

Webster, J., & Watson, R. T. (2002). Analyzing the past to prepare for the future: Writing a literature review. *MIS Quarterly 26*(2), xiii–xxiii.

Wheaton, W. C. (1999). Real estate "cycles": Some fundamentals. *Real Estate Economics 27*(2), 183-387.

Woods, M., Paulus, T., Atkins, D. P., & Macklin, R. (2016). Advancing qualitative research using Qualitative Data Analysis Software (QDAS)? Reviewing potential versus practice in published studies using ATLAS.ti and NVivo, 1994–2013. *Social Science Computer Review, 34*(5), 597–617. https://doi.org/10.1177/0894439315596311

MIX
Papier aus verantwortungsvollen Quellen
Paper from responsible sources
FSC® C105338

If you have any concerns about our products,
you can contact us on
ProductSafety@springernature.com

In case Publisher is established outside the EU,
the EU authorized representative is:
Springer Nature Customer Service Center GmbH
Europaplatz 3, 69115 Heidelberg, Germany

Printed by Libri Plureos GmbH
in Hamburg, Germany